LadyUp

*A Woman's Guide to
Self-Defined Grace and Fearless Love*

Wanda Marie

For information about permission to reproduce selections from this manual and any supplemental or supporting documents, write to:

Legacy Lifestyles LLC
PO Box 874
Skyland, NC 28776
Email: CoachWandaMarie@gmail.com
www.CoachWandaMarie.com
www.LadyUpNetwork.com

ISBN: 978-0-9797215-5-7

Contents

Acknowledgments

A special "Thank You" to those Ladies who loved, supported and walked with me through the entire first year of developing this work.

You are my Sister Queens and true Ladies.

Deborah Kagan

Janet Nichols

Jennifer Lanning

Melissa Webb

Ms. Venita

Rebecca Le Vine

Tara Thomas

Feminine Mystique

By Wanda Marie

Honor me and I shall receive you unto heaven,
into my holy temple of birth and rebirth,

into the sacred place of the most high,
into the fertile void of all creation.

As you rest inside me, I shall set you free,
free of your pains and worries, free from death,
for I grant to you through all that I am,
eternal youth, vitality, and longevity.

As you leave my side, you carry with you
my essence, my love, my life.
And you wonder why I become
protective, aggressive, possessive.

I can still feel you inside me, and I long to care for you,
to nurture you, as we have now become one.
Nurturing you is how I am nurtured;
this is my reason for being.

Life for those who dishonor my virtue
find pain and suffering to be an unwanted companion.
Life for those who honor me shall always be free,
for I am the Divine Feminine,

Feminine Mystique.

Introduction

Most women were taught how to be a lady, but few were taught how to remain a lady when anger or hurt strikes. We often turn into women with bigger balls than men. Over the years, I have observed a few of my close female friends become hurt, angry, and pissed off – through it all, they remained in their power as true ladies. I think we need more powerful ladies than pissed-off women. It's time to LadyUp! In order to help women LadyUp, I've developed this self-guided workbook based on my experiences as a long-time Women's Empowerment Coach and Trainer. It's about to get 100% REAL with who we are as women and get clear on what we really want!

It's been said that our DNA has not changed in more than 10,000 years. If this is true, women are still wired to gather, and men are still wired to hunt. Women go shopping to fulfill this instinct. However, many men are frowned upon if they want to go hunting. They therefore seek different ways to express their masculinity, and some of those ways are not favorable to many women. Men have lost their place, so women have basically taken charge while asking men to Man-Up! But how do they do this in a way that fits into their design as men while pleasing modern-day women? When we, as empowered women, step back and become the Lady, it's easier for men to man-up and be a man. Now, I'm not talking about women dumbing down so men can feel more respected – it's all about women creating the space for men to be who they were meant to be – for themselves and for the women! Keep reading – you'll get it!

Words have meaning, and words are powerful! Look at these words closely...

WoMAN

WoMEN

FeMALE

sHE

HEr

I guess when God created woman by taking a rib from Adam, this became our nature. We are a man with a womb, a wo-man. Well I've got another word for you that's all ours and does not belong to men, and it's called...

LADY!

The Evolution of Female

Princess

~~Goddess~~

Woman

~~Queen~~

We've been confused. We start out as playful little girls and, if born into a traditional American family, we become little princesses given everything our heart desires and looking forward to that fairytale life. When we get older and realize the fairytale is a lie, we jump from Princess to Woman. Even though our mothers try to teach us as girls how to become ladies, once the fairytale vanishes, we go straight into "I am woman, hear me roar."

The Goddess gets bypassed.
The Queen is never realized.

So as a woman, or wo-man, we start standing up for ourselves because the princess is dead since the knight in shining armor never showed up. We must now fend for ourselves! Be strong, work hard, and don't depend on any man. In fact, "I can do anything a man can do, and sometimes better! Who needs a man anyway?!" I hear this often from powerful women.

We become subconsciously resentful of men because of the lost dream, the disappointment in life, the abandonment, etc. We become so strong that we are often perceived by men as cold, unapproachable, or even bitchy.

And we get stuck on being wo-man. We become powerful women. Not a bad thing, but...

When does the Princess get to be the Goddess or
the Queen? And where does the Lady fit in?

We must learn to embrace those missing parts of our evolution, the Goddess and the Queen. But first, let's have a "Wanda Marie definition" of the various qualities of the feminine.

PRINCESS – *a young female, playful, innocent, often seen as a damsel in distress, usually a dreamer, and very creative.*

GODDESS – *a female, more mature than the Princess, but with similar qualities. She is charming and carefree. She can be very seductive in getting her needs met. She is accommodating and compassionate, she is a healer, and is often very loving and trusting of others.*

QUEEN – *a mystical and magical, highly respected mature female who knows her truth, and so lives her truth that she can command her world through simple gestures. She can shape-shift from Princess to Goddess to Queen, all in a matter of seconds. She is mysterious and powerful. She is a leader and tolerates little. Her love is undeniable and unmeasurable. She will love you and protect you, or quite easily destroy you should you betray her trust and her love. She is a real LADY.*

Princess
Goddess
~~Woman~~
Queen

BUT WHAT ABOUT WOMAN?

WOMAN – *a female who is great at multitasking, usually very controlling, wanting things to be done right. She is a wo-man and uses masculine effort to get things done, so she is often tired and stressed out. She's a teacher and can be very motherly. Because she is the caretaker, she has very little time for herself. She is a fighter and a survivor, not through grace, but through struggle.*

Society has taught us and programmed us to become women. It's time that we learn what it feels like to be respected as and treated like Ladies.

It takes a lot of skill and practice to become a Queen. It takes clarity, confidence, and courage. You must be willing to know your truth, speak your truth, and stand in your truth. It takes time and patience to get there. As you become more clear and confident, those around you will have to catch up. You will need to be patient with them and not chop off their heads as they are learning how best to serve you, the Queen.

Once a female has gained her crown, if hurt, disappointment, or anger finds her, she makes a conscious decision to act rather than react. She decides the next step with precision and the decision usually comes very quickly. It's either off with their heads, or they are pushed outside of the queen's court until allowed back in. Both treatments are more painful than any sort of acting out a princess might demonstrate, or any revenge a goddess or a woman might conjure up.

The reason a Queen's punishment is worse than any other is because her love and devotion is more powerful than any other. She will serve, nurture, and protect you, all at the same time. Once you have done wrong, that energy is deflected away from you and the void felt is tremendous. Most will do almost anything to get back into the good graces of a true Queen.

When you CARE about someone,
what's important to them
becomes important to you.

When you LOVE someone,
what's important to them
becomes a priority to you.

When you are IN LOVE with someone,
they become your priority.

5

Use Your Magic Wand &
Make the World a Better Place

Chapter 1
Keep Calm and LadyUp!

Time: Own Your Time
Order: Organize Your Life
Beauty: Create Your World

Chapter 1: Keep Calm and LadyUp!

My full definition of a Lady is someone who possess the qualities of both the Goddess and the Queen. She is more than a woman – she is a female with self-defined grace and fearless love. She is clear, kind, and loving yet protective and powerful. She is focused yet flexible. She has learned to set clear boundaries, raise her standards, speak her truth, AND get her needs met without slaying the dragon. She will love you like you've never been loved before, yet take you to your knees with a mere glance. She honors her values and walks in grace with unyielding gratitude for her life and the world which she has created from within.

Why be a Lady? Many women live out their entire lives in unhappy toxic relationships – relationships where they are not honored and are often taken for granted. This must stop with us if our daughters and granddaughters are to be happier and live fulfilled lives. We are the ones to change the dynamics of male-female relationships. If we can do this, I truly believe we can change the world. It takes a Lady, a Queen, to change the world, but it takes more than one. It takes more than a village – it takes a global community. If you're reading this, you are part of this amazing global community for change. Welcome, and thanks for joining the sisterhood.

The relationship we forge with others has a huge impact on our level of happiness and success in the world. How we relate to others determines how they respond back to us and it ultimately affects our experiences in life. How we relate to family, friends, colleagues, employers, employees, and others is important. However, my goal through this writing is to help shift how we relate to men and how they respond back to us as Ladies. To do this, we must first take a look at the most important relationship of all, and that's how we relate to ourselves as wo-men.

We must learn how to be a powerful Lady and allow the space necessary for a man to be a man. It's nice to have that masculine energy to look up to, someone who can handle a Goddess and a Queen, someone who is ready, willing, and able to be the provider, the protector. When someone like that has your back, you know it.

> *A high-maintenance woman is not a woman who wants a lot – it's a woman who does not know what she wants.*

Today, many men don't know how to be with a powerful woman; thus the term, "high-maintenance" became popular. A high-maintenance woman is a woman who does not know herself or what she wants or needs to be happy. Most men simply want to please their woman. If a woman does not know herself, it's hard for a man or anyone to please her. She is forever unhappy, and so is her partner, and the relationship suffers.

Self-Assessment

Want to become more of a Lady, a Goddess-Queen? Here's a little self-assessment for you:

1. Do you have healthy boundaries?

2. Do you articulate your boundaries clearly yet gracefully?

3. Do you stand firmly when your boundaries are crossed?

4. Do you raise your standards each year (*nice birthday gift to yourself*)?

5. Do you ask for what you want or need without shame or guilt?

6. Do you receive gifts and compliments with grace, ease, and gratitude?

7. Do you give to and serve others from your heart's desire rather than obligation?

How did you do? If you answered "yes" to at least 5 of 7, you did great! If you answered "no" to 4 or more, you are probably a real woman who works very hard with little or no acknowledgement or appreciation from others. You are probably unhappy and not fulfilling your purpose/mission in life. No worries; just keep calm. I'll show you how to LadyUp!

We have a Queen within us at every age. We were born with Queen qualities. How many times have you seen a two-year old acting as though she owns the world? We think it's cute until she reaches 16 and is still acting like she owns the world. Regardless of age, we all have the Queen qualities within us. However, if you want to identify at what age these qualities tend to become more prominent in our lives, it might look something like this:

Ages 0 to 20 is **The Princess:** Full of innocence and questions – the Receiver

Ages 20 to 40 is **The Goddess:** Full of fun and adventure – the Pleaser

Ages 40 to 65 is **The Queen:** Full of knowledge and vision – the Leader

Ages 65 to 80 is **The Wise Elder:** Full of insight and wisdom – the Peacemaker

Age 80+ is **The Mystic:** Full of Light – the Transcender

As a woman moves from Goddess toward becoming a Queen, there are major shifts that occur between being a "Pleaser" and becoming a "Leader" which can often be referred to as "a dark night of the soul," "mid-life crisis," or "menopause." Whatever you choose to call it, it is not comfortable. Women say it's hard to find their way. Some women never feel like leaders, yet this Queen energy is within them waiting to be expressed, waiting for them to find their purpose and their passion – for this is where they shall rule.

The Many Qualities of The Feminine

Pleaser Goddess Qualities	Leader Queen Qualities	LADY The Goddess-Queen
Intuitive/Personal	**Intellectual/Logical**	**Wisdom/Oneness**
Spiritual Insights	**Ground Rules**	**Mystical**
- Adaptability	- Stability	**Knowing without Reason**
- Spontaneous	- Structured	- Embodies and presents the Goddess or Queen energy depending on what is called for in any given moment or situation.
- In the Moment	- Mission Driven	
- Flexible	- Boundaries	
- Graceful	- Controlled	
- Service	- Leadership	- Divinity
- Inviting	- Commanding	- Space
- Honesty	- Loyalty	
- Comforter/Nurturer	- Warrior/Protector	
- Healer	- Teacher	
- Dreamer/Creator	- Builder/Destroyer	
- Playful/Inspire	- Serious/Motivate	
- Order and Beauty	- Function and Results	
- Process	- Completion	
- Open & Receptive	- Cautious/Generous	
- Authentic	- Confident	

Becoming a Lady Is a Spiritual Journey

A Lady Needs 3 Things
Time, Order and Beauty

Time: Own Your Time

When you are rushed, you become a woman getting things done with masculine energy. A lady takes her time and does things with grace and ease. No, it's not always practical to take your time, but we often find ourselves rushing when it's just not necessary. **Be consciously aware of when you are rushed without reason.** Plan your year, your month, your weeks, your days, and down to the hours. Yes, life happens and yes, I know the saying, "Man plans and God laughs." But, when you don't have a plan of your own, you will often find yourself at the beck and call of someone else's plan for you. Then we bitch and complain about how unfair life is. Try to put some perspective on the quality of your time – don't waste it. You can spend money and get it back. You can't get back the time you spend – spend your time wisely. It helps when you place a dollar value to your time. Professionals (doctors, lawyers, service providers, etc.) charge for their time by the hour. How much is your time worth? There is no wrong answer. Your time could be $25 per hour or $25,000 per hour. What matters is that you believe you are worth what you say.

EXERCISE: Close your eyes and play the numbers game with me. Say to yourself, "I can honestly accept what my time is worth, and today the dollar value I easily place on my time is $_____ per hour."

Fill in the blank with different figures until you find one that feels good to you. You will know it's right because you won't be afraid to tell someone or to charge someone that amount. If you feel uncomfortable stating your price, it's not the right price for you, no matter how badly you want it to be. If the consciousness is not there yet, you're fooling yourself and it won't work. Get real and accept what's right for you in this moment, today. If you're not happy with your number, do this exercise again and again and again, week after week after week, until your level of acceptance meets your level of consciousness and it feels good. When it begins to feel like it's not enough money, and you know you deserve more, that's when it's time to raise your number (hourly rate and fees), so do this exercise again at that time.

Your time is your most precious commodity; don't misuse it or give it away without conscious consideration. Be kind to yourself – you're a Queen!

When you organize your time wisely, you create more order in your life and less drama. Learn to **anticipate the outcomes of your decisions**. When you say "yes" to something, be aware of what you are saying "no" to. When you say "no" to something, be conscious of what you are saying "yes" to. Keep in mind how **your choices today create your tomorrows**.

EXERCISE: Think of a situation where you are spending a lot of time doing something you don't want to do. Now ask yourself these questions:

1. How do I feel when I'm doing _____?

2. What's the cost to me? What's the cost to others around me (*do ya get a little bitchy*)?

3. How is continuing to do this serving me *(mental stimulation, emotional attention, etc.)*? (*We all receive some sort of benefit from everything we do.*) What's the benefit? And, can I get that same benefit in a different way or from a different person?

4. Who can do this for me? (*Women try to do it all while Ladies/Queens delegate and leverage their time and energy in order to serve more people.*)

5. What can I do to change this situation and when? (*Create light at the end of a dark tunnel.*)

6. If this can't be changed right now, what needs to happen for me to accept the situation more gracefully?

THINGS THAT NEED TO BE DONE **THIS YEAR**

1. Get job in HR field. (Make more $$)

2. Try volunteering/making connections to get into counciling

3. volunteer w/ out of Darkness

4. _____

5. _____

THINGS THAT NEED TO BE DONE **THIS MONTH**

1. _____

2. _____

3. _____

4. _____

5. _____

THINGS TO BE DONE **THIS WEEK**

1. _____

2. _____

3. _____

4. _____

5. _____

THINGS TO BE DONE **TODAY**

1. _____

2. _____

3. _____

4. _____

5. _____

Order: Organize Your Life

Order is about how you organize your life, your home, your closets, and your drawers as well as your time and your resources. When your home, your car, and your surroundings are in order, life is more graceful because you save time not having to constantly look for what's missing. You know where things are, as every item has a place. Get organized and release the clutter!

EXERCISE:

1. Week 1: Clean out all of your dresser drawers. If you have not worn/used an item in the past year, let it go. Make three piles: (1) Give away, (2) Throw away, and (3) Sell.

2. Week 2: Clean out all of your closets and create the same three piles.

3. Week 3: Clean out any attic, garage, or storage unit, making the same three piles.

4. Week 4: Take immediate action to get rid of those piles. Don't procrastinate! Do it NOW!

Even though it feels good to create more space, know that it's in our nature as women to want to fill a void. Be consciously aware of this and figure out a way to manage the urge to clutter again. If I buy a dress, I discard a dress to maintain the space and the balance. Form a healthy habit of letting go of stuff you don't need. That habit will eventually become your nature, and you will find that you begin to also let go of emotional baggage you no longer need.

Order is a beautiful thing. It not only saves time, but physically, mentally, and emotionally you just feel better, lighter, and healthier. You may work your butt off like a real woman to get this done, but in the end, you will breathe better, relax, and feel more like a Lady. When you feel more like a Lady and carry yourself like a Lady, people will begin to treat you that way.

Take a lesson from <u>Marie Kondo:</u> "Tidy your space and transform your life." Visit her site at <u>www.konmari.com</u>.

Beauty: Create Your World

Beauty is sacred. It's magical. It's nature's way of touching our soul and reminding us that we are connected, that we are all one. People travel for miles and miles to see the wonders of the world. The breathtaking views never cease to amaze us – mountains, streams, rivers, oceans, rolling hills, valleys filled with wildflowers. The one thing that most can agree upon is that Mother Nature provides us with heavenly artwork – stunning and amazing beauty!

Women are deeply connected to Mother Nature as evidenced by our menstrual cycles. Men are forever trying to understand and conquer women and Mother Nature by climbing the highest mountains and diving the deepest seas. <u>The feminine need not conquer</u> that which she is. She is Mother Nature in human form. She is destined to create beauty.

When you don't take the time to stop and smell the roses, and acknowledge the beauty surrounding you, you are ignoring a large part of what connects you to nature. It is nature that heals and reveals through you. It is nature that creates the magic in your world. It is not man, but nature that brings forth your guidance and protection.

Many indigenous cultures around the world understand the power and the magic of Mother Nature. Although men recognize the beauty and the awe, most can't connect as we do. Most women taking on male roles in relationships have lost touch with this powerful force of nature. Yet, there are still a few modern-day mystics among us carrying the torch and bearing the light.

The feminine is like the sun, made to shine brightly. The masculine is like the moon which gets its light from the sun, from the feminine. When we don't shine, the world becomes a very dark place. Ask any man how he feels when his woman has gone silent. He can't handle the silence, so he desperately tries to fix it! Can you see how important it is for you to connect to nature, to beauty, to be the light and to shine? It's not just for you — we shine to light up the world, to create a better world for everyone.

What sparks you and makes you shine? What makes you smile inside? What do you see with your eyes that touches your soul? Is it flowers, a newborn baby, puppies, kittens, a landscape, sunset, ocean waves, rolling hills? I'm specifically asking, **what things catch your attention and put an involuntary smile on your face?** These things may change over time depending on where you are in life and what you're going through. But for today, just for today, what does it for you?

I love looking at trees. I moved to the mountains in North Carolina for the trees. We bought a piece of property that had a few amazing trees and one was diseased and had to be cut down and removed. At that time, I had no idea how painful it would be for me to watch that process. When the arborist's chainsaw started cutting the tree, I burst into tears and broke down sobbing. I was shocked at the effect it had on me. The trees speak to me. They hold the wisdom of the ages and I have only begun to listen. Trees touch my soul with their beauty. The way they dance in the cool breeze at twilight soothes my soul and brings me home to myself.

Where there is a sense of beauty, there tends to be more peace and calm. The feminine is a natural channel for beauty to flow. We were born to create beautiful spaces, to turn houses into homes. Yet, we as women don't always have the time to allow for the creative juices to flow. We are too busy making a living and taking care of everyone else. Even if you are a single parent, it is imperative for you to take time for yourself. Take time to open your creative channels and allow the beauty to flow through you, as *you.*

When women allow beauty to be an important part of their lives, they begin to attract beauty. When they attract beauty, they begin to feel more beautiful. When they feel more beautiful, they walk differently, speak differently, and become more attractive in every way. They become more ladylike – more graceful, warm, and approachable.

EXERCISE No. 1: Color your world beautiful. Create beauty all around you. Start with these five spaces:

1. where you eat

2. where you sleep

3. where you bathe/shower

4. your personal vehicle

5. your personal workspace

Do something special for each space to make it more beautiful, more you. Maybe add fresh flowers or candles. Maybe drape a scarf over a lamp shade to change the lighting in the bedroom. Maybe add photos to your workspace that bring you joy and make you smile. I don't mention the living room because, unless you live alone, this space is often shared with others and carries a lot of different energies. The spaces mentioned are usually the spaces where women freely set the tone and vibration they desire. You are a Lady filled with creative juices. Allow the creativity to flow through you out into your world.

EXERCISE No. 2: If you've done a good share of personal growth work in the past, you may have done some mirror work. I'm asking you to do it again, but take it deeper than ever before.

Look in the mirror and say to yourself:

"I am one with Mother Nature. I am beautiful inside and out. I see beauty all around me. I create beauty all around me. I lovingly radiate this beauty through me to everything and everyone around me."

Repeat this process over and over again until you can really FEEL it deep inside. Some women have been known to shed tears once they begin to feel the power of this process. Allow yourself to look deeply into your own eyes. Reach down into your soul and touch the beauty that is you.

Chapter 1 – Keep Calm and LadyUp
Personal Assessment

Time: Own Your Time

_____ I allow myself space by creating time buffers on each side of all events and tasks.

_____ I am clear about the dollar value I place on my time.

_____ I no longer have the disease to please.

_____ I put me first and productivity and results second.

_____ Time is a man-made concept; I've learned to expand and collapse time to serve me.

_____ I no longer allow people to waste my precious time.

_____ I no longer apologize for making myself a priority.

_____ Instead of being sorry, I now appreciate people who wait for me.

_____ I declare that everything happens for me in Divine Timing.

_____ Every week I'm delegating and eliminating at least one activity I don't like doing.

Order: Organize Your Life

_____ I have a clear vision of how my environment will look and feel on all levels.

_____ I no longer demand anything of anyone; I make requests and I command my world.

_____ I no longer struggle to get things done – I call forth "Divine Order."

_____ I trust the process of life completely.

_____ I have no clutter in or around my home, car, or workspace.

_____ All of my papers are filed away (no unopened bills).

_____ All of my finances are in order (I also have a Living Trust/Will).

_____ All of my relationships are healthy (family, friends, and associates).

Beauty: Create Your World

_____ I know that I'm deeply connected with the beauty of Mother Nature.

_____ I know that I'm beautiful, so I'm starting to attract more beauty into my life.

_____ I allow beauty to flow through me with grace and ease, however it wants to show up.

_____ I have created beauty where I eat, sleep, shower, my workspace and my vehicle.

I own my time, have order in my life and I create beauty in my world. I do this with clarity, confidence and courage. I have an amazing life.

Notes to ponder and share with others

"I Live an Amazing Life"

I am blessed to be able to do what I want,
when I want, and how I want.
I do what I love and love what I do for a living.
Life is good and this is easy.

Chapter 2
Braving Your Passion

Reveal Your Truth
Release the Stories
Turn Passion to Profits

Unclear Passion

By Wanda Marie

Simple days and silent nights where fantasies and daydreams run wild and free.

Not knowing what to say but needing desperately to speak, I find myself with mixed emotions and abstract thoughts. Needing to understand but not wanting to know.

Seeing only black and white for colors become confusing, as shades of who we are seem to clutter the clarity we need so much to hold on to.

Molehills become mountains in the midst of dramatized simplicity, and safety becomes lost in a fog as creativity surrenders itself to expectations.

I can't stop thinking about you, your strength carefully displayed through your tenderness. Your curious smile and caring eyes keep me enchanted with who you are. I don't want to change you – I long to know you.

Dear God, help me to see clearly that which I fear. Help us to understand our union, to embrace the power and express the passion, the passion to live life more freely, more creatively, more lovingly.

Because right now, my only possession is unclear passion.

Chapter 2: Braving Your Passion

Passion is raw. It's that part of you that exits through and beyond your physical limitations. It is beyond the ability of the mind to comprehend. The closest term I can use to define passion is a state of absolute and pure bliss. You can't identify it within the bounds of time and space.

When your passion is ignited, you cease to be the personality you know yourself to be. You are no longer governed by ego. You surrender to and become one with the cosmos.

Whether your passion stems from making love, painting a picture, or creating a piece of music, it all comes from the same space inside of you – the red root chakra, the survival instinct, the energy around the tailbone area. When this energy force is set in motion and allowed to soar, it not only creates, and procreates, but it can move mountains. It rises from the tailbone area up through and around your spine and out the top of your head, through the transpersonal point of your being, which some might call heaven.

This dynamic creative force of nature often frightens women, so we keep it on lock-down. We keep it safely tucked away so as not to harm, hurt, or surprise anyone with our power, our magnificence. We will, however, allow it to bring forth a child into the world. A slight clue as to our magnificence! We will also sometimes allow ourselves single, and sometimes multiple, small bursts of pleasure called orgasms. And even then, we don't always fully let go and surrender. When trusted, this powerful creative force can be directed to not only heal you, but to help you manifest your dreams.

That root chakra energy is where your passion begins. And for most, that's where it ends. Unless we're practicing Tantric Sex, we're allowing this passion to blast through in a fast and quick moment of ecstasy where many call out, *"Oh God...I'm Coming!"* And, then it's over and we're back in control and feeling safe again. As a side note, Tantric sex is considered an enlightened path to higher consciousness. One of my favorite books from way back is, *"Jewel in the Lotus"* by Sunyata Saraswati.

You know you are in your passion when you are so focused on whatever you're doing that you totally lose track of time. **Passion is the driving force for your purpose, your mission** in life. It is the creative intelligence that brings your purpose into manifestation.

What are you so passionate about that when engaged, you lose track of time and forget that you are even on Planet Earth?

Are you willing to surrender, to let go, and **brave the wilderness of your passion**, allowing it to drive your purpose and your mission?

No one can join you in your passion. They can join you in your vision, your dreams, and your mission, but when it comes to the essence of passion, you become one with all that is, and in that space there is no other. Passion is an energy that fulfills itself. It needs nothing to complete itself. Another person can ignite our passion, but it is up to each of us to fully surrender to it and allow it to carry us.

There must be a sense of safety for most women to experience full-on passion in the bedroom and out into the world. What will it take for you to feel safe enough to surrender, to be free? When you trust that your passion will only lead you to the fulfillment of your deepest desires, it will be easier for you to surrender.

To live a passionate and purposeful life, you must:

1. Reveal your truth, getting brutally honest about your deepest desires,

2. Release the stories, the lies you've been telling yourself; and

3. Be willing to turn your passion into profits, allowing it to support you.

Reveal Your Truth

If you are to become a Lady, a Goddess-Queen, living with purpose and passion, you need to know your truth.

After years of studying with a wise teacher, she said to me, "truth is a lie." WHAT?! I needed to know what she meant by that since everything she had taught me was supposed to be about truth. She went on to say that what you believe to be true today is not so later on, as you evolve through life. She was right. What was true for me at age 25 was no longer the same truth at age 35 or 45 or 55. As we continue to grow and consciousness evolves, what we know changes. This is a good reason to avoid arguing for what you believe today, as it may change tomorrow.

One thing does not change, and that is our soul's purpose, our reason for being, the reason we incarnated on this planet. Why are you here? Don't say you don't know, because you do. You were born knowing. As we mature, we are influenced by the world around us, and what we know to be possible becomes more important than that which is unknown, yet is truly ours to do.

> *What we know to be possible becomes more important than that which is unknown, yet is truly ours to do.*

✳✳ Truth leaves clues. As a child, what did you want to become? What are the compliments you repeatedly received from people around you?

If you have truly forgotten why you're here, this exercise may help you to reconnect with your soul's purpose and rediscover your truth.

MEDITATION: You will need a mirror, a small candle, and your journal.

1. Sit up close to the mirror. Light the candle and place it between you and the mirror.

2. Recite this affirmative prayer: *"I give thanks for knowing my higher purpose and mission in life."*

3. Gaze just above the candle flame and into your eyes in the mirror. You may begin to notice your face morphing and that's okay. You may even see images behind you, and that's okay too. Just keep gazing into your own eyes while reciting the above prayer.

4. Only sit for 5 to 10 minutes at a time. You may receive insight the very first time or it may take several sittings before you are clear. Be patient with yourself and LISTEN for that still small voice that is always speaking to you and guiding you. LISTEN and take notes. Write down anything and everything that comes to mind. Don't judge it – just write it down.

VISUALIZATION: If meditation (sitting still and listening) is not for you, you may enjoy creative visualization where you are taken on an inner journey to receive more insight.

Most smartphones come with a voice recorder. If you don't have one, you can search and download a free app. Record yourself reading the following visualization exercise. You may want to read it a few times for practice before recording. Once you have the recording done, make sure you have your journal. Sit in a quiet place, take a few deep breaths, start the recording, close your eyes and just listen, taking it all in. When complete, journal your thoughts and feelings.

RECORD:

"I am from a planet far, far away. The place that I call home is beautiful, a place where there is no pain or suffering, no lack, and everything one would need is there in abundance.

But I can see there are other planets not so fortunate. One is called Earth. This planet appears darker in color, as though surrounded by a cloud. It has a much lower vibrational frequency than my own. There is a sun, but less bright. There is foliage, but dull and subdued. There are mountains, streams and oceans, but they are not healthy. There are plants and animals and yes, there are human beings.

I can see that the beings of Earth are not happy. They believe in lack and live in a constant state of survival. They fight to gain power over each other. I want to help. I want to show them a better way, I want to help them understand that they can raise the vibration of their planet, live without pain or suffering, and have an abundance of everything they need.

There are a million ways that I can help. I could inspire and influence them through music, or art, or even give them hope through medicine. I could teach them about human rights, God, science, and the universe. I could bring about law and order through the justice system. I could nurture and care for wounded and abused animals. I could advocate for and care for the planet at large.

There are so many ways I can help these people and this planet. I've had dreams, many, many dreams about how I could best serve this planet, yet I had forgotten. I'm now ready to remember my dreams. I'm ready to take action, to live my truth, to brave my passion. I'm ready to take responsibility and do what is mine to do. I may not know how, but I know that because of where I come from, everything and anything is possible, and I will be guided. All is given to those who ask. I now ask to know the way. I now ask to remember my dreams. I am passionate about helping, and I am brave enough to say "yes" to my passion."

*Remember to journal your thoughts and ideas
following the visualization.*

It takes courage to be ready to know your purpose. There are several reasons we don't want to know. **When we know the truth, we are expected to live up to it, step up our game, take responsibility for our lives, stop playing small, etc.**

When we are not following our truth, it eventually catches up with us and we become exhausted to the point of frustration and even illness. **Knowing our truth can be so scary, some would rather live out their life in pain and suffering, making that their mission rather than taking responsibility for their true purpose.**

When you are ready, fully ready to be healthy and happy, you will want to discover your reason for being, your purpose. And, you will do one or both of the exercises above.

*Am I truly ready to accept
the responsibilities of
my purpose, my mission?*

*I'm ready to face what
scares me?*

You may already know your higher purpose, but may be in such deep denial or fear, that you don't recognize it. Here are a few scenarios that may help you understand your own situation.

SCENARIO # 1 (Dentist)

I'm really good at what I do, but the truth is, I dream of having a farm, growing my own food, and living off the land.

I tell myself there's no money in living that way, and I have to make a decent living for the three kids that will be going off to college soon.

SCENARIO # 2 (Waitress)

I hate my job. The truth is, I just want to form a band, write original music, and have it played on all the radio stations across the nation.

My folks keep telling me to stop dreaming and go get a real job. I hear them, and I'm not sure that I can support myself doing what I really want to do.

SCENARIO # 3 (Housewife)

I love being able to stay home and take care of the family. And, the truth is, I dream of someday owning a retail store that sells my signature line of designer handbags. I keep telling myself this will never work because I have no experience in the retail market, and I have no desire to go back to school and learn.

There are so many scenarios, such as, I want to be a writer, I want to teach classes, I want to start my own spiritual center, I want to own and run an animal sanctuary, etc. What stories are you telling yourself to save you from doing your truth?

WHAT IS YOUR TRUTH? Write out your scenario:

1. What I tell myself is _____
_____

2. But the truth is _____
_____

Release the Stories

How have you been protecting yourself from your passion? What are the stories you've been telling yourself? What stories do you have spinning on "repeat"?

I am not smart enough to _____

I am not strong enough to _____

I am too old to _____

I don't have enough money to _____

I don't have enough time to _____

I need a partner to _____

I need to get healthy so I can _____

I need/want/don't have/wish I had _____
_____

Lies, lies and more lies we tell ourselves! I love Byron Katie's work when she asks very powerful questions. "Is it true?" "How do you know it's true?" **My question to you is, when did you start believing each story or lie?** And, are you ready to release those stories that are no longer serving you, and replace them with more empowering stories, ones that lead you to live an amazing life?

EXERCISE: Reverse every statement and turn it into a positive affirmation.

I am smart enough to _____

I am strong enough to _____

I am young enough to _____

I have enough money to _____

I have enough time to _____

I enjoy having a partner who _____

I am healthy enough to _____

All my needs are met, including _____

When I first met my husband, his story was that he had a bad back. Although there was never a problem when HE really wanted to do something or go somewhere. I began to notice a pattern. Whenever I wanted to go someplace that he was not too excited about, his back would conveniently go out. He unconsciously used his body to say "no" for him. This saved him from having to tell me the truth and risk hurting my feelings.

I later learned that years prior, he had been diagnosed with Epstein-Barr, so he thought he needed to preserve his energy or he would relapse. He preserved his energy by only doing things HE really wanted to do, and having his back say "no" for him when he didn't want to do something.

With some help and guidance, he learned that it was safe to just say "no" and I would not get angry or upset. His back has not gone out in the past 20 years to help him speak his truth.

> *I had to be lady enough to create the space for him to man-up and know his truth.*

I've worked with women who can't seem to lose weight. Some of their stories revealed that they needed the weight to feel safe. Men don't look at big girls, so it's safer. This is another lie that women tell themselves to hide from the truth. One woman wanted to quit smoking, but had trouble doing so. We discovered that smoking was the only time she could bond with co-workers during breaks. Even deeper, she discovered she also needed the smoking as "permission" to even take a break.

What is the biggest lie you've been telling yourself for years? What story have you claimed as your badge of honor, or badge of horror?

Whatever we are doing or going through that is not serving us on a higher level is serving us on a lower level, and there's a story behind it.

EXERCISE: In your journal, write it out:

1. What I've been telling myself is _____

   _____

2. And this has served me by _____

   and/or protected me from _____

3. My new story as of today will be _____

   _____

4. It's important for me to replace the old story now because _____

   _____

5. I am _____% committed to living my new truth.

Take a lesson from Byron Katie.
Watch a short Youtube video searching
"Byron Katie - The Work - The Essence in her own words."

Turn Passion to Profits

Once you know what you truly want, and you are willing to let go of the old stories that keep you small and safe, your next step is to create what I call your **Passion to Profit Plan.**

In the first chapter, we talked about the value of your time. It is important to revisit the notion that you are valuable – therefore, your time is valuable. What you choose to do with your time is up to you. You can sell yourself short by spending your time doing what you "think" you have to do to make money, or you can spend your precious time doing what you love AND make money. How much money? That depends on where your level of acceptance meets your level of consciousness. **This is your comfort zone.**

If you're doing your passion but it's not fully supporting you, you will need to consider your level of consciousness, your belief system. If anyone has ever been fully supported doing what you want to do, you can too. If you are breaking new ground, someone has to do it, so it may as well be you.

Another factor to consider is partnership. Every marriage or partnership, whether intimate or professional, has its own level of consciousness. You will balance each other out. This is huge, so be careful who you partner with in business. Most married couples will attract their opposite. One who enjoys spending money will usually attract a partner who enjoys saving money and vice versa.

Knowing your comfort zone, how much you can gracefully and easily accept for your talents or services, will help you understand where to begin. Don't begin at your comfort level; **begin just below your comfort level**. When you begin short, there is room for confidence-building. You KNOW you are worth more, so you won't hesitate to ask for the lesser amount. That level of confidence you've built up will also attract more business to you with less effort. As a Lady, you always welcome grace and ease in everything you do, including running a business.

For the sake of this wiring, let's assume your passion is leading you to start some type of business that provides a service, rather than operating a retail store. The following pages will provide you with a great deal of clarity for getting started.

Ready to Start a Business? Open your journal and answer these questions:

1. What do I really want to do and why now? What will it do for me?

2. What are my fears around doing this business? How do my fears serve or protect me?

3. Am I ready to let go of those fears? What would it be like without them?

4. How can I overcome my fears and take action now? *(List personal steps to be taken.)*

5. Do I have the support of family and friends? If not, where can I find a support system, brainstorming or mastermind group, or a business coach? *(Remember, no one ever succeeded alone.)*

6. Do I have a role model to follow or look up to? Who?

7. What do I want to call my business? *(There's a lot to be said in a name.)*

8. What will it take to get started?
   - Skill and knowledge
   - Time and energy
   - Money

9. What is motivating me? Is my passion driving my purpose? Is the vision pulling me?

10. How many reasons do I have to succeed?

11. What will be my business image?
    - Sweet, loving and caring
    - Honest, hardworking with integrity
    - Firm, direct and confident
    - Comfortable and easygoing
    - Professional and high-profile

    (Incorporate all the characteristics of a business you admire.)

12. Where will I conduct my business? Private space in my home? Rent/lease an office, share an office space, work for someone else?

13. What will I need to get started, and what about start-up costs?
    - Business cards, letterhead, and envelopes
    - Website, merchant account, shopping cart
    - Equipment needed: computer, business phone, answering service
    - P.O. Box address
    - Business licenses and permits
    - Errors and omissions insurance
    - DBA *(for a fictitious business name)*
    - Business bank account – checking account
    - Business credit card *(don't mix business with personal)*

14. What do I estimate the monthly cost of operating my business will be (expenses)?
    - Webmaster/website maintenance
    - Marketing *(10% to 15%)*
    - Rent/lease office
    - Utilities
    - Postage
    - Office supplies
    - Other

15. What is the total amount of my current financial obligations each month *(personal expenses)?*
    - Rent/mortgage
    - Utilities
    - Car payment/insurance
    - Health insurance premiums
    - Childcare
    - Loans
    - Other

Keep Going! Freedom is in Your Hands

Don't Get Discouraged with Laying the Foundation

16. How much money do I need each month to pay all my personal and business expenses?

    Formula for what you need to charge:

    How many HOURS a day do I want to work? (*target not more than 4 hours a day*) _____

    How many DAYS a week do I want to work? (*target not more than 3 days a week*) _____

    Multiply the number of hours you want to work each day by the number of days you want to work each week for a total number of hours per week you will be working.

- *4 hours a day x 3 days a week = 12 hours per week*
- *Multiply the 12 hours per week by 4 weeks (one month).*
- *Equals 48 hours per month to work*

To find your breakeven point, divide the number of work hours into the total amount of expenses (personal and business):

Example: *$3600 a month expenses divided by 48 work hours per month = $75 per hour which is the minimum you can charge per hour and break even.*

$75 per hour x 48 hours per month = $3600 per month which covers your expenses (personal and business)

17. How many clients/customers can I service in an hour? (*Set your schedule accordingly.*)

To make a profit, you will need to increase your price per hour, or increase the number of hours you work, or increase the number of people you see in an hour by doing group work.

Find out what the highest prices are being charged for what you do and find a place just below your personal comfort zone to start. But remember, people don't trust prices too low!

Always pay the Queen first. Put at least 10% of every dollar that goes through your hands into your personal savings account!

Ask yourself, "What can I do to keep costs to a minimum?"

- Make trade agreements and barter for services you need.

- Barter with printers and others who can help you cut down on costs.

- Share an office with someone whose business will complement yours so you can refer each other clients/customers.

- Always try to share advertising costs with someone, for this can be your most expensive investment.

- o Use email and social media advertising; it is free or costs very little.

- o With so much spam in emails, snail mail is making a comeback! Use it wisely.

- o Mail out announcements on postcards rather than flyers to save on postage.

A good place to start would be to hire a business coach or mentor. For free business planning assistance, contact SCORE at www.score.org.

Creativity Running Wild!

On a final note, the female energy IS creative. This means the creative juices flow through you, as *you*, and you may be the receiver of multiple creative ideas! Do you do them all? Do you focus on one or two? Do you put all of your energy into one project at a time?

You must remember to follow your passion; it leads you to fulfill your purpose. You are not passionate about all those ideas separately. Look closely – how many of the ideas you're receiving have a common thread? Find the commonality and you will be led to your true passion. Then, you can decide to follow one path, or get creative and combine all of them.

Once your purpose is being fed, you will have the energy to do many other wonderful things. If you don't put your purpose first, all the other great and wonderful ideas will take time and drain your energy rather than feed you.

The barometer for knowing your passion is that you would do it regardless of being paid, and you're not happy unless you're doing it.

It's time for you to brave your passion. Trust that it will set you free. A passionate Lady leading a passionate life can command anything she wants in her world with grace and ease.

Chapter 2 – Braving Your Passion

Personal Assessment

Truth: Reveal Your Truth

_____ I am willing to know the truth of my passion.

_____ I'm not afraid; I look forward to braving the wilderness of my passion.

_____ I have learned to control my passion and turn it on and off as needed.

_____ I am totally honest about my deepest desires.

_____ I don't need outside stimulation or drama to feel alive or important.

Stories: Release the Stories

_____ I am willing to grow beyond the negative stories I've been telling myself.

_____ I have released all the stories that no longer serve my truth.

_____ When negative thoughts arise from old stories, I now remember the truth.

_____ I can easily see/imagine myself more successful than ever before.

_____ I can expand my comfort zone to include the entire world.

_____ I'm learning to feel safe in my body and comfortable in my world.

Profit: Turn Passion to Profits

_____ I know what it takes, and I'm willing to take risks.

_____ I am ready to earn more to serve more.

_____ I value my time and I'm not afraid to charge for it.

_____ I realize that I AM the gift, and what I offer is the icing on the cake.

_____ I have a business plan for my passion to create or increase my profits.

_____ I allow my passion to drive my purpose and my profits; they are one.

Notes to ponder and share with others

Chapter 3
Allowing Grace

Awareness: Beyond Thought
Connection: Universal Intelligence
Trust: Intuitive Knowing

Welcome Grace

By Wanda Marie

Invite Grace to tea.
She'll bring you a gift, one you cannot see.
A silent friend called Ease,
whose joy is only meant to please.

You cannot have one without the other.
Grace and Ease are sister and brother.

You may argue with Grace not to take away your pain,
for you think, in the pain is your greatest gain.

Ease enters but is quickly pushed aside,
for the hard path you've chosen is designed to seduce pride.

Why has Grace come for tea? The invitation was merely a
courtesy? And now there's Ease, invading your privacy.

It's time for Grace and Ease to leave,
Or you can change your mind and start to believe.

Life is more fun and such a breeze when you have tea with Grace
and Ease.

Chapter 3: Allowing Grace

Let's start with the LadyUp version of grace. It can be summed up in one word—"EASY." Our goal is to make life easy for ourselves and our loved ones, and we will do whatever it takes to make this happen. In order for life to be grace-filled and easy, we have to stop struggling. We have to be willing to release the drama that's so stimulating, that makes us feel so alive. This drama makes us feel needed by others and gives our lives false meaning. We have to be willing to allow grace to work its magic in our lives.

Grace is not something that's earned or learned. It's there for everyone—we just have to be made aware of it, connect with it, and trust the process.

In order to lead a life more attuned to grace, we have to learn to listen to and trust our intuition, that part of ourselves that so many of us neglect, that part that is as natural as breathing and as amazing as the heartbeat. To get the most from this chapter, I encourage you to come to this teaching like an innocent child, with an open mind, curious about the unknown, and above all, willing to grow beyond what you think you know.

Believe it or not, we were born filled with grace. Grace is that God-given presence within us that watches over us, takes care of us, and carries us through difficult times. Most people call upon the grace of God when in trouble, pain, or a difficult situation. They ask for mercy, but they often feel undeserving of such mercy.

We were born with grace but have since learned struggle. We have identified so long with struggle that we have come to believe that it is a natural part of life. We think that miracles are special and not the norm. Everyday miracles are possible for those who live in grace. A miracle is that place where logic ends and magic begins. The logical mind could never comprehend the Grace of God and the miracles that manifest moment to moment as a result.

You are reading this because some part of you believes there is a better way to live, and you are tired of struggling. You want that magical life that you know exists. Your first step is to become aware that there is something bigger than your ego that serves you. Then, you will move on to consciously connect with it through your intuition, and finally you will learn to trust it without reason.

You've probably heard about the Law of Attraction. This law says that through our consciousness, we attract what we believe. So, if we believe we are loved, we will attract love. Believe that we are wealthy, and we will attract more wealth, etc. This is the power of the subconscious mind at work.

> *Beyond the Law of Attraction is Grace.*

Grace goes beyond the Law of Attraction. In order to attract something, we must acknowledge that it is separate from us. This sense of separation is the greatest cause of suffering. **Grace heals the separation, and all we need to do is set our intention and trust our intuition.** That's how we learn that we are the genie in the bottle we've been wishing would appear. So show up! Show OUT! Surrender to grace and live an amazing and magical life.

Grace is a sense of ease and freedom. We have been programmed to be busy and productive, and we have forgotten what ease feels like. If the conscious mind is not busy enough, we tend to unconsciously create something to do. Often, we create problems to solve, which creates drama. The cure for this is to allow more grace into our lives. **This is done through awareness, connection, and trust.**

Awareness: Beyond Thought

Awareness is stillness and observation. It's about becoming aware of that which is beyond our thoughts. To become more aware, we must tune in through some type of meditative process, causing the mind to be still and enter the silence. Fine-tuning and aligning our energy centers, also known as chakras, is a meditative process that serves not only to open us up to universal wisdom and knowledge, but to create that space of stillness and silence for expanded awareness.

At an early age, I was able to hear the whispers of Spirit in the wind. I wasn't hearing voices, and I don't recall words. I was "sensing" what was right and what was wrong. Sometimes the feelings were so strong, I would argue for what I believed to be true. As I grew older, I came to understand that even though everyone has the ability to hear the whispers of Spirit, not everyone is aware. I then learned to listen for others and became a Channeler, providing guidance to those who were unable to hear for themselves.

I later wrote down my process for being able to listen and hear what Spirit was saying, and created a training manual, "***Flying with Angels: Learning to Channel.***" For years, I taught others to channel for themselves. Here's a practice activity I offered to help people move beyond personal thoughts to receive spiritual guidance. Please read through the entire exercise first, and then proceed.

1. Find someone to work with you who you trust, and who is open to "playing." Ask your partner to prepare a question ahead of time but not to share the question with you yet. It should be about something that is important to them and for which they would truly like some guidance. It should not be a question that requires a simple "yes" or "no" answer, but a deeper, open-ended question.

2. Get into a meditative state by taking a few deep breaths and relaxing (eyes open or closed). *(Optional but powerful: Follow the process on*

the next page for aligning your chakras to get connected to universal intelligence.)

3. When you feel calm and centered, have your partner ask you the prepared question.

4. If the question is not clear, you can ask for more details, but you are not allowed to say, "I don't know," because you *will* know – just trust your deep intuition.

5. Start your answer with, "***What I'm getting is that ……***" and just start allowing information to flow through you without filtering, without judgement. In order to have the information flow freely, it may help to speak faster than normal, not giving your conscious mind a chance to filter. Just let whatever comes forth to come out as a steady stream of consciousness.

6. Invite your partner to take the best and leave the rest – no judgment!

This is a great way to practice getting still to become aware of what you're feeling and to move beyond your thoughts. It is important to remember that, although the question is serious, this is still a practice exercise, and you are not responsible for the information or what your partner does with the information. Make sure to present this disclaimer prior to playing.

To Practice Awareness in the Moment:

• Practice feeling what an object feels like before you touch it.

• Practice tasting food in your mind before it goes into your mouth.

Connection: Universal Intelligence

Lady up network — Something about chakras?

Connection is about sensing and knowing what's right for you. To learn to connect, you can't be afraid of being vulnerable or open. Being open leads to trust. Don't confuse feelings with emotions, or feelings with fear.

One of the best ways to connect with Universal Intelligence and expand your awareness is to open, clear, and align your chakras, the 7 major energy centers that run through your body.

Set the intention

THE 7 MAJOR ENERGY CENTERS (Chakras)

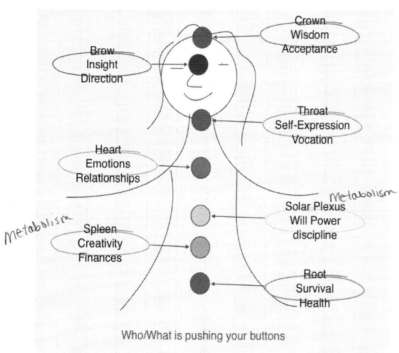

Crown
Wisdom
Acceptance

Brow
Insight
Direction

Throat
Self-Expression
Vocation

Heart
Emotions
Relationships

Metabolism
Solar Plexus
Will Power
discipline

Metabolism
Spleen
Creativity
Finances

Root
Survival
Health

Who/What is pushing your buttons

When we open these centers, we are opening the portal to universal intelligence. This opening stimulates us and communicates with us through our intuition.

Our intuition lies in our gut, somewhere between the spleen chakra and the solar plexus chakra.

Sit and meditate on each of these centers, one at a time, starting at the lower one. Visualize them spinning in a counterclockwise motion, opening up. **This is fine-tuning your chakras**. Then visualize a beam of white light running

[handwritten note at top: ~~ Lady up Network = is about fine-tuning and strengthing my intuition and making it work for us to make my/our life easier.]

from above the crown down through the root and into the core of the earth. **This is aligning your chakras** to create a clear and open channel for information and insights to come through to you.

You are now connected to that Universal Intelligence that even guides and directs the planets.

Intuition is alive and well in everyone. We must learn to **become more aware, connect, and trust** the process.

1. Awareness is to open our senses to that which is beyond our thoughts.

2. Connection is to be still and truly sense what we are feeling intuitively.

3. Trust is to know you are truly guided to make only the best decisions.

What would having this type of awareness, connection, and trust do for your relationships, your business, your work, your creativity, and your amazing life?

EXERCISE

✳ **Practice Connection in the moment:** What feels good, what feels bad, what feels neutral? To be clear, assign qualities to these sensations. Here are some examples that work for me:

[handwritten note: My Good = Green, Check mark ✓ sweet taste in mouth, Sound of chimes (pretty wind chimes) My Bad = Red, "x" mark, hot ears]

- **Good** = sweet, warm, green, etc.

- **Bad** = sour, cold, red, etc.

- **Neutral** = salty, moist, blue, etc.

Decide for yourself what qualities you will assign to the various sensations. Ponder a situation you are facing. Become still and **expand your awareness** to include all your options. **Get connected** so you may feel and sense which options are best for you. When you are open, aware, and connected, your intuition speaks loudly. **Follow your gut!**

The more connected you are, the more intuitive you become and the better your intuition can serve you.

There are four main areas of life: **Health, Wealth, Love** and **Happiness**.

4 tires, all inflated.

#4 • **Health** encompasses the condition of the physical body and your environment.

#1 • **Wealth** covers finances, career, creativity, and mental stability.

#2 • **Love** deals with emotional issues, family matters, romance, and sexuality.

#3 • **Happiness** focuses on your core beliefs and spirituality.

Decide which one area needs the most attention in your life right now and focus on that area for one week. Then move on to the next area in need of the most attention. Then cycle back around again, spending more time in the areas needed.

YOUR DAILY PRACTICE

- Know what area of life/issue you want to focus on.

- Set a timer to sit for 10–15 minutes.

- Get still and move into the silence.

- Fine-tune and align your chakras to connect with universal intelligence. *Clear + spin them counter clockwise*

- Ask for guidance from beyond your own thoughts.

✳ • Be still and know. Expect intuitive insights.

✳ • Journal whatever comes through (thoughts, ideas, images, etc.).

At the end of each week, look back and note how many times you followed your intuition. Each week you should be following your intuition more and more – trusting more and more.

Trust: Intuitive Knowing

Trust happens when you are not controlled by fear. Trusting is a choice we make daily, moment to moment. To trust, we must develop our intuition to a point where trust comes naturally. Once we trust ourselves, no one can ever rob us of our power.

Trust is demonstrated by acting upon your intuition:

- Practice Awareness. Feel the results of your choices before you make them.
- Practice Connection. Notice how the results feel intuitively (good, bad, or neutral).
- Follow your Intuition: Trust that you are making the best decision.

Intuition doesn't always hit us in the gut. When you are open, you could hear voices or sudden sounds, or you might see images that have meaning for you. Learn to trust what feels good and right.

It's easier to trust your intuition when there's a deeper understanding of what it is and how it works.

WHAT IS INTUITION?

Intuition is the ability to acquire knowledge without the use of reason. It's like a sixth sense. Everyone has it, but few choose to use it. It's like the elephant in the room that everyone chooses to ignore. Thought of as "too woo-woo" because it's not as tangible as the other five senses (sight, sound, smell, taste, and touch).

Only those who delve into the psychic realms are expected to explore and develop this sixth sense. The average person is expected to deny or ignore this amazing phenomena that is a living, breathing part of who we are. Yet, many successful businessmen and women attribute their success to following their intuition. Many artists and musicians rely upon intuition as a guide for creative expression.

HOW DOES INTUITION WORK?

The word 'intuition' comes from the Latin word *intueri*, which is often translated as meaning "to look inside" or "to contemplate."

Scientifically Speaking: Scientists say our subconscious mind absorbs every tiny detail we encounter as well as every one of our experiences. It sees, records, and stores every subtle unit of information that the conscious mind does not pick up. Therefore, when making decisions, if we only rely upon the conscious mind for answers, we are missing valuable information that has been gathered by and stored within the subconscious.

Just as the heart knows how to beat, when to beat, and how many times per minute to beat to keep us alive, so does the subconscious mind know exactly how to gather, record, and store important information that is vital to our health, safety, and well-being. It's a built-in survival mechanism that extends beyond our individual safety. It is designed to protect the human race and move the species forward.

The subconscious mind communicates and tries to guide us through feelings and impressions. During dream state, while the conscious mind is resting, the subconscious is most active. This is one reason it's important to pay attention to our dreams. **Albert Einstein received the theory of relativity in a dream.** I think he was paying attention!

Spiritually Speaking: Spirituality teaches us that it is through our intuition that God speaks to us and guides us. So, when we pray for answers and have faith, answers come by way of intuition, the ability to know without reason.

Whether there is a supernatural deity responding to our prayers, or the subconscious mind simply doing its job, just like the beating heart, I think we can all agree that there is something that looks over us. It guides us, tries to keep us safe and helps us become more successful if we would but listen and trust. And, whatever it is that's providing such guidance, it's truly beyond the comprehension of our conscious reasoning mind.

When we are listening to, trusting, and following our intuition, we usually do the right thing and not only do we win, but those around us win as well. Imagine if we could get the entire world doing the right thing!

The first step is to reestablish and strengthen our connection to that universal intelligence some call God or Spirit. Then we must be willing to listen, learn to trust it, and follow its guidance. The link that makes the connection possible is our feelings. **Not our thoughts**, not the thinking mind, not our intellect or logic, but our gut feelings.

The umbilical cord to Spirit is never severed. We are always nurtured through this feeling deep down in our gut, our instincts and our knowingness.

We always pay a price when we ignore our gut feelings. But, because we live in a world where so often, **more value is placed on logic than instinct**, we have learned to ignore our gut and follow our heads. BIG MISTAKE!

It's typically easier for men to follow logic as they are wired to be linear thinkers to focus for the hunt. Women are not; we are the multitaskers and gatherers with diffused awareness, wired for expansion in all directions. This includes having greater access to our feelings.

Through a willingness to combine intuition and reason, intuitive people appear to have some life advantage. Edith Jurka, M.D. says, "Intuitive persons have a sense of more ultimate control and advantages in life because intuition and right-brain functioning add creativity, humor, and the ability to solve problems, to reach goals, and to manage people more effectively."

Now aren't you glad you're among the smarter folks by learning to lean into and trust your intuition? It's not only a good thing, but it's a powerful way of living.

Learning to Trust

One of the ways you can learn to trust your intuition is to simply acknowledge when you are right. Often, we say to ourselves, "something told me to..." This is the voice of intuition. Even if you didn't follow it, acknowledge that it was there and give thanks for the awareness. Something was trying to offer guidance – be grateful.

At other times, you know something to be true, but you doubt. Learning to trust often means being still and observing before you jump in. Allow whatever is happening to simply unfold. Then you will know you were onto something. When we jump in and speak too soon, we often find we're off the mark. Intellect interferes. Wait for it, be patient, allow whatever is happening to reveal itself and you will find that you were right.

Beware of the ego. So often when we start hitting the target consistently, we get a big head and start thinking we always know what's right. Nothing shuts down the connection faster than ego taking over. Be humble in that which you come to know, and handle your wisdom with responsibility.

Here are a few fun guessing games you can play that will help to develop your intuition.

1. **The Card Game:** Shuffle and place a regular deck of cards in a stack face down on a table in front of you.

    -   Close your eyes, get still, ask to be connected by saying, "I am open and clear."

    -   Set a conscious agreement with your intuition that the red cards are a lot warmer than the black cards.

- Place your non-dominant hand over the stack of cards, just above the deck, not touching, but just enough space between your hand and the deck for energy to flow through.

- Ask your intuition to tell you the color of the top card by creating a warm sensation if it's red, and a cooler sensation if it's a black card.

- Once you feel the energy, turn the card over for verification. Create two piles of turned over cards, one for those you got right, and a separate pile for those you have to guess again.

- Once you move through the entire deck, take the stack of cards you did not get right, shuffle them and repeat the exercise with just those cards.

2. **Red Light, Green Light:** Make a conscious agreement with your intuition that red means "no" or "stop" and green means "yes" or "go." Agree that there will be a small flash of red or green color that moves swiftly through your awareness according to truth. It helps to practice first with bright red and green flash/index cards.

- Close your eyes and get centered.

- Now make statements which you know are true, such as, "My name is…." And watch for a green flash of color. Declare true facts about your age, where you live, what colors you are wearing, etc., and continue watching for flashes of green.

- Then make statements which you know are NOT true. Cover different falsehoods to get a sense of the red light flashing before your awareness.

- Once you get it, no matter how soft the light, move on to speaking about things that can't be known yet, but will become verifiable. Such as, "I will get a call from _____ today." See what proves true.

3. **Keep Guessing:**

- Guess how many pieces of mail will be in the mailbox before you open it.
- Guess who's calling before you look at the phone.
- Guess what color your friend will be wearing when you see her.

4. Think up your own fun guessing games that will help develop your intuition.

> *"I never came upon any of my discoveries through the process of rational thinking." — Albert Einstein*

Your intuition is always working for you. Sometimes you listen, but most of the time you don't because (1) you're too busy to stop and really listen, or (2) you haven't learned to trust it completely. The only way you will learn to trust it is to use it. The more you use it, the more accurate you will become at discernment, and the more useful your intuition will become for guiding you to having an amazing life.

The goal is to have your whole life guided by your intuition each and every day – to actually have a conscious experience of this awareness, connection, and trust in your relationships, your work, your business, your creativity, and your entire life!

Chapter 3 – Allowing Grace

Personal Assessment

Awareness: Beyond Thought

_____ I get that grace does not have to be earned or learned, only allowed.

_____ I have fully accepted grace as my way of being in the world.

_____ I have learned how to channel awareness beyond my own thoughts.

_____ I have practiced "Awareness in the Moment."

_____ I am totally ready to live a grace-filled life without the rush of drama.

Connection: Universal Intelligence

_____ I know how to connect to Universal Intelligence at any given moment for my answers.

_____ I trust this Universal Intelligence to guide and direct my life.

_____ I know how to fine-tune and align my energy centers (chakras).

_____ I can clearly identify what feels "good" and what feels "bad" before making decisions.

_____ I have a daily practice that keeps me connected to Universal Intelligence.

Trust: Intuitive Knowing

_____ I am committed to setting my intention and following intuition.

_____ I practice trusting and following my intuition daily.

_____ I know that intuition is the ability to acquire knowledge without reason, and I trust this.

_____ Whether it's my subconscious guiding me or Spirit, I trust what I get.

_____ As I grow in intuitive knowing, I handle this power with wisdom and responsibility.

Notes to ponder and share with others

Chapter 4
Embracing Your Body

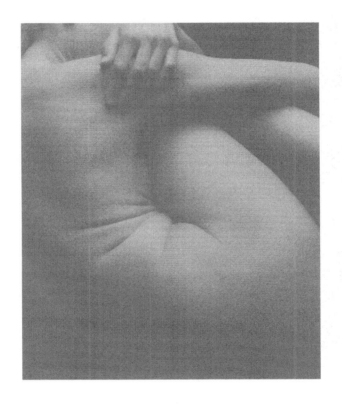

Eyes Wide Open
Acknowledge Imperfect Perfection
Be Willing to Be Seen

I Apologize, I Love You

By Wanda Marie

Dear Body,

You have been beaten down and dragged around
with little or no respect to be found.
I apologize, I love you.

You carried my child for months at least nine,
I blessed the gift and cursed the stretch marks left behind.
I apologize, I love you.

You've carried me through all the heartbreaks and pain,
He left me for another and upon you I placed the blame.
With each teardrop I hated you and called you names.
I apologize, I love you.

I've stretched your quart-sized stomach to fill my own void,
then I punish and deprive you for being overweight.
I fed you things you didn't want or like in preparation for a date.
I apologize, I love you.

Over the years I celebrate how I've changed and grown,
Yet the changes you've gone through I negate and even hate.
I think it's because of you that I've lost my way and can't relate.
I apologize, I love you.

Dear Body, In times of wanting to end it all, I never appreciated
all that you've given. I've disrespected you, put you down,
shamed you, called you names and even at times have been
shamed by you. And yet, you continue to carry me.
Please forgive me. I apologize, and I love you.

Chapter 4: Embracing Your Body

Oh my, such a touchy subject for most women. For those of you who know me well, you know that I like to greet myself each morning with, "Hello, Beautiful." I've got enough ego going on that this is usually quite easy for me. However, it is difficult to remember to do it each day. I soon came to realize I would only say this when I actually felt beautiful. That had to change because I KNOW that when we change our mind, everything else follows. So I started saying, "Hello, Beautiful" when I looked like shit in the mornings. Funny thing happened, there were less and less mornings where I looked like shit. I started actually believing I was beautiful. That new attitude carried me through my day. How would your day be different if you left the house each morning feeling beautiful?

I got so excited about feeling beautiful, regardless of what the lying mirror was trying to say, that I began saying "Hello, Beautiful" to some of my female friends when answering the phone. Most of the time, they didn't know how to respond. I have one friend that responds, "Hello, More Beautiful." I love that, even though I realize she's not fully embracing the compliment, just throwing it back to me.

To embrace your body is to honor your body. Yes, I've heard it all, "Beauty is only skin deep," "Beauty is in the eyes of the beholder," "It's what's inside that counts," etc. Let's face it ladies. The cosmetic industry is not one of the most lucrative industries in the world because of those phrases.

According to a 2017 article in Forbes, "It's never been a better time to be a beauty entrepreneur. Forbes estimates that there are at least 40 prominent beauty startups today founded by women, making the $445 billion (sales) industry one of the most prevalent places for women to self-start their way to big-time success." According to Orbis Research, "The global cosmetic products market was valued at USD $532.43 billion in 2017 and is expected to reach a market value of USD $805.61 billion by 2023."

HELLO
Beautiful

I use a facial cleanser and toner, and I moisturize. Other than that, frankly, I'm too lazy to deal with putting on and taking off makeup. When I'm feeling frisky and put on a little makeup, people are shocked and wonder why I don't wear it all the time. It's just not me.

I had the "makeup" conversation with a close girlfriend who shared with me that putting on her makeup is like meditation for her. It's a joy and makes her feel like a lady. I was stunned – I always thought putting it on was a chore. So, I tried the joy approach. Didn't work for me; it was still a chore!

It doesn't matter if you wear makeup or not. What does matter is if you do wear makeup, what's your WHY? Are you wearing it because you enjoy the process of applying it – brings out the artist in you? Are you wearing it because it enhances the joy of being female, or are you wearing it because that's the only way you can feel beautiful?

For so long, we have allowed the media to tell us what is beautiful, and we have all failed to measure up. The models on television have been starved and made up in ways that the average woman would never have the time or resources to pull off to look that glamorous every day. Even though women only make up about 20% behind the scenes as directors, writers, and producers, we have made progress. Thank God the media is changing. Have you noticed we're seeing not only more full-figured women on film and television, but we're also seeing more mature women as leading ladies? And, we're starting to see more men in domestic roles in commercials, cleaning the house, changing diapers, and doing the laundry. Ladies, there's hope!

In order for us to truly see ourselves as we want others to see us, we have to get real. We have to open our eyes and see what's really there, acknowledge that what we are is perfect, and then be willing for others to see us as we truly are – Absolutely Beautiful!

Eyes Wide Open

What do you want to see when you look at your body? What do you actually see? What if I told you that what you see is what your mind has been programmed to see. And, you can change the programming to see differently.

ASSIGNMENT: If you haven't seen the comedy, "**I Feel Pretty**" starring Amy Schumer, watch it. If you have seen it, watch it again!

The movie brilliantly demonstrates the power of the subconscious mind and how we see ourselves that then determines our behaviors and actions in the world, and ultimately impacts our level of success.

Yes, you may already know this, but I want you to FEEL this. I want you to be willing to look at yourself and choose to see differently. Make up your mind that you are the one who gets to decide how others will see you and treat you.

I want you, as a Lady, to be in charge of your world, and the way you carry yourself is a large part of how you will be able to take control of your court as a Queen.

When you walk with your head held high, shoulders back, and a long stride, people will take notice and wonder, who is that Lady? They will be curious, and you will begin to attract interesting people in your life.

Another great movie is "**Last Holiday**" starring Queen Latifah. This movie also demonstrates what happens when you show up differently and how the world treats you accordingly.

EXERCISE: When you're ready to open your eyes, here's an exercise that will help you begin the process of embracing your body. Romanticize and heal your body to energize your life.

1. Take yourself on a date, home alone. If it's impossible to find some alone time at home, take yourself to a nice hotel for the night and just get away.

2. Bring along some scented candles and flowers and your favorite soothing body lotions, or pamper yourself with an amazing Body Butter. Don't worry, I'm not going to ask you to pleasure yourself, but it is optional if the mood moves you☺. Nice, soft music is wonderful, but instrumental only – no words to distract you. Have a hand mirror nearby for later.

3. Remove all clothing and reveal your lovely body. You can shower beforehand if you prefer, but it's not necessary.

4. Strategically place your flowers so you can see them when you get comfortable. Light your candles, get comfortable on the bed, the floor, or the chair, so that you can massage your feet.

5. Begin to massage your feet with your body lotion, spending at least one minute on each foot. As you massage, thank your feet for all they do and have done for you. Apologize for any abuse you've caused, such as wearing uncomfortable shoes, running too hard, walking too much, dancing too long, etc. You may need to apologize for simply standing on your feet too long and working all day. End the foot massage by saying, "I see you, I love you."

6. Then move up to your calves and knees. Massage them, apologize for any stress you've caused them, and thank them for carrying you all these years. End each portion of your body massage the same way, by saying, "I see you, I love you."

7. Stand and rub your thighs, hips, and buttocks, spending at least 30 seconds on each area. End the same way, "I see you, I love you."

8. Now it's time to lie down and focus on your belly. Allow your attention to penetrate and massage all of your internal organs, sending healing energy, loving them. End this portion the same way, by saying, "I see you, I love you."

9. Bring your awareness to your female reproductive system, healing and loving your sacred womb. End this portion by saying, "I *feel* you, I love you."

10. Gently spread your legs apart and lovingly massage the mound of Venus, the vulva, outer layers of the vagina. Pick up your hand mirror and look at this amazing place of both pleasure and sometimes pain. Adore the fact that you are female and you are amazing. Apologize for

any abuse that you may have done, allowed to be done, or had no control over what has been done to this part of you. Let your female parts know, "I see you, I love you."

11. Set your mirror aside, and begin to massage your chest (your heart) and your breasts, again spending at least 30 seconds on each area. Apologize for any abuse you or someone else may have caused and end this section by saying, "I feel you, I love you."

12. Massage one shoulder, down the arm, and then the hand and fingertips. Then switch and do the other shoulder, arm, hand, and fingers, end by saying, "I see you, I love you."

13. Massage your neck (release who/what has been a pain in the neck for you), and end by saying, "I feel you, I love you."

14. Massage your face (how have you dishonored your own face?), paying extra attention to your lips (what have you said, who have you kissed), gently caress your ears (what have you heard that tore you down). Pick up your hand mirror, look into your eyes, and say, "I apologize for any abuse that I may have done, allowed to be done, or had no control over what has been done to you. Thank you for being so strong, beautiful, and amazing. I see you, I know you, and I love you."

15. Put down your mirror and begin to massage your scalp (brain) and end by saying "I feel you, I love you."

16. Stroke your head, your hair thoroughly and end by saying, "I feel you, I love you."

17. Now scan your entire body, head to toe, and see if any part of your body needs extra love and attention. If so, return to that part and repeat the process for that part. Shower yourself with love and admiration – you deserve it!!! And, you don't need to wait for someone else to give this to you.

Once you have completed your full body massage, slowly repeat this mantra over and over until you drift off into a wonderful twilight sleep to awaken at the precise time you tell yourself you want to wake up. This could be a 10-minute rest, or an overnight deep sleep – you get to decide.

Mantra: *"I love you, I see you, and I adore you."*

Acknowledge Imperfect Perfection

I recall a powerful life-changing dream I had in my early twenties.

I was walking down the middle of a small-town street with cars parked along the street to my right. I happened to notice an elderly woman walking in the same direction, but on the sidewalk, on the other side of the parked cars. She was old and haggard looking with dirty, torn, and I assumed smelly clothing. She was carrying lots of bags of all sizes. I also assumed she was a homeless person.

When I looked over at her above the parked cars, she looked at me and our eyes locked for a moment. Fear welled up inside of me. She dropped her bags, moved between the parked cars, and started to cross into the street where I was walking. I picked up my speed and walked between the cars to get onto the sidewalk as she was entering the street. I looked back, and she had disappeared.

I got down on the ground to look underneath the cars, to see if I could see her feet to determine her proximity to me. As I looked under the cars, she was there! She grabbed hold of the clothing on my shoulders. I pulled back and stood up as quickly as possible. She was clinging so tightly to me that when I stood up, I pulled her up from underneath the car with me. There we were, face-to-face!

She looked deep into my eyes and I instantly saw my mother's eyes. As she gazed deeper, I then saw myself as her, I could feel our oneness. She put her arms around me and embraced me, holding me tightly. Tears started flowing as I could not contain the intensity of the love I was feeling. It felt like my soul was going to explode. I woke up.

That was the beginning of my impulse to hug everyone. I'm a true hugger. When I hug someone, I'm reaching to embrace their soul. When you can embrace someone's soul, you come to realize that we are all one. All the judgments slip away into oneness. It's beyond love. It's just is-ness. We can do that for each other. We can take someone beyond love if we can get past the body, the judgments – if we can get past our own body insecurities, imperfections, and judgments.

The woman in my dreams was not perfect by any means. However, what she gave me was beyond perfect. I call this imperfect perfection. When you look at yourself in the mirror, do you see perfection according to the standards society has set for us? I don't think so – we are our own worst critics. But what if you created your own standards and acknowledged that there may be things you'd like to shape up or change, but it's all perfect right here and right now, because it's all you?

Again, in my early twenties, when I did the majority of my personal growth work, I was blessed to have children with a man (*husband number one*) who adored me and my body. When we met, I was 17, cute, hot, and sexy. That was not the case as he observed me in the delivery room. Legs spread wide, shouting obscenities, a bloody mess and a big head of hair making its way out of my vagina. In the moment, I didn't care about how I looked or who was looking. I just wanted that kid out! But then, there was the episiotomy *(an incision made in the perineum — the tissue between the vaginal opening and the anus)* which was performed because the kid was huge and it's better to have this procedure rather than have your vagina ripped to shreds. So the healing process is not only painful, but prolonged for weeks after delivery. For weeks, I felt like shit and looked like shit, and couldn't have sex! Every day, this man would reassure me that I was beautiful to him. Even though I didn't believe it, I needed to hear it. It was imperfect perfection. If we hear something long enough, we eventually start to receive it, then we come to know it for ourselves and own it. I am beautiful no matter what the mirror says. I own my beauty. What needs to happen or be said for you to own your beauty?

EXERCISE:

1. Find someone you trust — it could be a friend (male or female), a partner, a sibling, a parent — anyone you trust to help you with this exercise.

2. Have them say to you, "you are beautiful," every time you speak by phone or see each other. They will forget, but make an agreement that it's okay to gently remind them.

3. Each time you hear it, pause and take in a deep breath. Receive it at first without words.

4. Watch how well you receive this compliment. Pay attention to your emotions and your physical body language. Then simply say, "thank you." No need to return the compliment. When we offer up a

compliment after receiving one, it's often our way of deflecting the energy we don't think we deserve.

Practice until you can honestly receive the compliment and simply respond by saying, "thank you" with a smile and mean it, without having to return or justify the gift.

Be Willing to Be Seen

I learned about being vulnerable and humble at an early age and in a variety of ways. One of the most positive experiences was while attending modeling school. There we had to do commercials that got us out of our comfort zones. First, they build up your confidence by teaching you and making you look great on stage. Then they throw you on stage alone and make you look like a fool. It was great training for what life does to us all. I recall being alone on stage in front of the entire class and being asked to create a commercial, impromptu, with me sitting on the toilet and selling toilet tissue. I was humiliated, but I did it, and I did a great job. This was strange for me because I often had reoccurring dreams of being exposed while going to the bathroom. It's a shitty feeling!

There are times and places where you never want to be seen! However, in most of our waking hours, it is important to be acknowledged by others. We have a need for acceptance, and until we are willing to be seen, we won't be acknowledged or accepted.

What keeps us hiding is usually our insecurities about the way we are being perceived in the world. It may be the way we look, the way we speak, lack of education, or even our culture can keep us hiding out as women.

India Arie reminds us that you too are a Queen. Listen to the lyrics of the song "Video"! This Queen, during her recent tour, including a stop here in Asheville, NC, starts the concert with a beautiful head of hair, and ends the concert revealing her beautiful bald head to show that she is not her hair! We all must be willing to be seen for who we really are.

The War Is Not Over

One morning while having breakfast with hubby, a Vietnam vet, we were looking out over our lush jungle-like backyard and admiring the beauty of the grounds and all the trees. He reminded me that when we first moved here to the mountains, he would have bad memories. Not flashbacks, but the foliage here brought back memories of being on the frontline in the jungle in combat. He said, "You never knew where the enemy might pop up, and you had to be on guard constantly." One day, the good news arrived for him that the war was over. But, in the minds of many who fought in the war, the trauma would haunt them for years to come.

I told him this is what it's like for many women who've been raped. The war is never over. The female is wired to look to the male as provider, protector. When your protector abuses you, you learn to protect yourself, you become a hard-ass woman and you no longer trust anyone, especially men.

The difference in being in war is that you have an idea of where the enemy lives and you are prepared for battle. As a woman, no one prepares you to protect yourself, and you don't know who the enemy is or where he lives. And, if you are the one-in-five women who have experienced sexual assault by a man, you may be living in a constate state of fear. Your mind may be preoccupied when you walk down the street — are men watching you? If so, how does this make you feel — sexy or scary? In the grocery store, at the gym, everywhere you go, you are being watched. Walking to your car alone at night with keys in hand, on high alert. The war is not over for those women. In combat, the fighting eventually ends with one side winning and one side losing. In the male/female relationship, if the female loses, there are no winners.

So how do we heal the wounded female? How do we help her to feel safe enough to want to be seen, to want to shine, willing to dance in the moonlight with others, not just alone. We don't have to trust men, or anyone, but we do have to trust whatever God is for you. Without a spiritual foundation, we are lost. Following a spiritual path is the quickest way to healing the pain of the past. This takes us back to the chapter on "Allowing Grace." Learning to listen to your intuition will keep you safe, guide you, and protect you. Do your inner work, your daily meditation and stay prayed up. You will come to trust the process of life, regardless of your past. You will begin to notice you are always at the right place at the right time. You will begin to find that all your needs are met before you know you need them. The more you come to trust Spirit and your spiritual practice, the more comfortable you will become in your body and the easier it will be for you to enjoy being seen. You will want to shine and bring joy to others by allowing them to witness the beauty of your dancing in your divinity.

> *It is truly a dark planet when women are not shining their light. We owe it to ourselves and we owe it to the world*
>
> ***TO SHINE, AND TO BE SEEN.***

Chapter 4 – Embracing Your Body

Personal Assessment

Eyes Wide Open:

_____ I love up on my body daily!

_____ I see my beauty through my smiling eyes each morning in the mirror.

_____ I can say, "Hello, Beautiful" and mean it each morning.

_____ I see me, and I like me, a lot!

Acknowledge Imperfect Perfection:

_____ I get that I may not look like a model and I'm okay with that.

_____ I have scars that contribute to my character and my beauty.

_____ My body is unique, and I am blessed because of it.

_____ I have someone in my life who tells me "You're beautiful."

Be Willing to Be Seen:

_____ I use my mantra often: "I love you, I see you, and I adore you."

_____ I'm willing to be seen without being all made up.

_____ I'm willing to allow others to see me when I need to ask for help.

_____ I'm willing to be seen as powerful, beautiful, and successful.

> _I am beautiful, I am perfect, and I am enough._
> _I am healthy. I am whole and complete!_

Notes to ponder and share with others

Chapter 5
Mystical Manifestation

Shift from Goddess to Queen
Use Your Magic Wand
Be the Power You Possess

You Are the World

By Wanda Marie

You are the SUNSHINE when the world seems cold-hearted,
Your kindness and gifts of love are to be rewarded.
You are the world.

You are the MOON always seeming to change,
When in reality always remaining the same.
You are the world.

You are the STARS each so similar yet unique,
The beauty in others, you forever seek.
You are the world.

You are the RAIN nicely scattered,
Honoring other's beliefs while remaining unshattered.
You are the world.

You are the RIVERS extending deep and wide,
In you, it's easy to confide.
You are the world.

You are the WIND that sets birds free,
This personal freedom, your forgotten reality.
Just a reminder – You are the world.

You are the BEGINNING and the END,
Soon you will understand there really is no sin.
For You are the world.

We are one in this amazing UNIVERSE,
The one you love, the one you curse.
Yes, WE are the world.

The world we've created together, for we are one.

Chapter 5: Mystical Manifestation

Eight years old and I wanted a red bicycle so badly I didn't know what to do! Mama was a hard-working nurse in Los Angeles who worked the graveyard shift, so I lived with my grandparents in San Diego, Big Mama and Big Daddy. Every kid on the block had a bike. I would watch them ride by our house in envy. Mama couldn't afford to get me a bike and Big Mama and Big Daddy preferred I didn't have one for fear of my safety.

I began imagining myself riding with the other kids as they flew by. I would close my eyes and I could feel the breeze on my face. I even saw myself riding with no hands! Let's back up – I had never been on a bicycle so I had no idea what it would feel like to ride one, or if riding with no hands was even possible for me. But I wanted to know, and I wanted it badly. Every day after school, I would see the other kids and I would imagine myself riding with them.

Christmas came and the guy mama was dating wanted to impress her by buying her daughter a bicycle. It was blue, not red, and it was so big, I could hardly get onto the seat. It had no training wheels, so I stumbled and fell down a lot while learning to ride. As a young adult studying metaphysics and universal laws, I realized, that as a child with a wild imagination, I had manifested that bicycle. It was my creative imagination that brought the bicycle into my reality, even though I had not imagined it with much detail. It was blue, not red, and I didn't know I needed a small bike with training wheels. Yet, I had put so much energy and feeling into riding a bike, it had no choice but to become my reality – despite all circumstances.

Was creating that bicycle a mystical event? Not when you understand the power of the subconscious mind and universal laws. Universal laws are as precise as gravity. What goes up MUST come down. What you put out into the universe MUST come back to you. Your subconscious mind is a powerful computer and will make manifest from the data you input. The **data is derived from energy plus conviction**. Energy comes from your conscious thoughts, what you focus on. Energy flows where your attention goes on a regular basis. Conviction comes from what you feel inside when focused.

> *Your feelings create the fuel that moves the energy (thoughts) forward into manifestation.*

I quickly learned how to get up on the bike, ride it, and eventually ride with no hands. I mastered that big blue bike! I felt the breeze upon my face, just as I had imagined!

I had a vivid imagination, as most children do, but the intense feeling of riding that bike made it so real that it had to show up in reality. As adults, we tend to lose that vision. Helen Keller said the only thing worse than being blind is having sight but no vision.

Everything in the universe is mystical until we understand it. I've always been very aware of patterns in the world. I often see grid lines that others don't see. I've seen right through objects. Once, I was standing and waiting for an elevator. As I stood there gazing at the doors, the doors began to move and morph. I began to see the structure the doors were made of. I could see inside the doors, the nuts and bolts, the steel posts, everything inside the doors. I had the thought that I could actually, at that moment, put my hand right through the door like in the movie *Ghost*. The thought frightened me and yanked me back to this reality, this world. I tend to block out the energy grids and shut down this sixth sense because it's distracting when trying to navigate the physical world and be "real."

I've always known that the world we see with our outer eyes is just a microcosm of what really exists. We all must learn to see beyond this world, and into the many other dimensions of time and space. Once we are able to utilize more of our brain power and psychic energy to do this, we will laugh at how easy it is to manifest our heart's desires.

I have never believed in gurus. I think we are our own guru. Yet, one night I had a dream of an orange dump truck, and lots of orange garbage bags. The dream repeated itself for several nights straight. My spiritual teacher at the time told me that Sai Baba (Satya Sai Baba), an Indian guru who always wore orange, was working with me, removing psychic garbage from me. My thought was, okay, whatever. Later that week, the manager of my apartment building, whom I had only said maybe three words to ever, knocked on my door and presented me with a framed photo. He said, "This is a picture of Sai Baba and he wanted me to give this to you." It was a very old wooden frame and photo. Taped to the back was an old piece of paper neatly folded to hold the ash that was contained inside. The paper was covered with Hindu writings/prayers. I later learned that the ash inside was considered holy ash, called vibuthi. I was told that the vibuthi could be used like holy water, for prayer and healing and that it would always replenish itself. This was more than 25 years ago, and I still have the wood-framed photo and some of the original vibuthi.

I have moved several times over the years and that photo of Sai Baba always ends up in my home office. I don't believe in gurus, but I know my dreams and the photo showing up was no coincidence. Since Sai Baba's death in 2011, there have been many who say he was a fraud, but I know that his presence has blessed me. **He was considered a Spiritual Scientist**. He knew how to use his mind and psychic energy to manifest his world. He was known for manifesting holy ash, rings and other jewelry from thin air and giving them to people for healing. Thousands have claimed he healed them. Thousands also claimed that Jesus healed them. In the Bible, Matthew 9:28–29 it says, "When he entered the house, the blind men came to him, and Jesus said to them, '**Do you believe** that I am able to do this?' They said to him, 'Yes, Lord.' Then he touched their eyes, saying, '**According to your faith be it done to you**.'" So you may believe in Sai Baba or Jesus or Buddha, but the real healer is you! Remember, YOU are the world. What heals you is your "faith." Sometimes I place my faith in Advil. What about you? ☺

What this boils down to is the fact that you can manifest whatever you believe is possible. The big question is, what do you believe is possible for you? I ask this of clients who want to make a change. I ask, "What do you really want?" Most of the time, they limit their desires to the capacity of their will. They find it easier to want something they know they can have or achieve. Use your imagination, expand your vision, believe in yourself, and feel the intensity of your desires! Name it, claim it, and own it!

> *The clarity of your consciousness and the intensity of your feelings create your world. Remember: YOU Are the World.*

The clarity of your consciousness and the intensity of your feelings create your world. The reason this is mystical is because most people have a very hard time understanding it and believing in it. Your feelings fuel your intention (inner-tension) to light your creative fire. When you can say, "I want _____ and I KNOW it is ALREADY mine," you will have it. There is a feeling that goes with declaring it's "already mine" or "already done." You can't waiver, you must be super-clear. You must know it with conviction. There must be a "NOO" (No Other Option) attitude. I name it, I claim it, I own it! Done!

> ### *Mystical Manifestation =*
> *I Name It ~ I Claim It ~ I Own It! DONE!*

A word of caution here. You never want to impose your will upon another person. You should never name, claim, or own another person. You can name, claim, and own the qualities you desire in a person, but you can't force someone to be that for you. For example: You want your partner to be emotionally available, loving, spiritual, generous, etc. You have named it, claimed it, and owned this relationship experience for yourself. You simply focus on being with "someone" with those qualities, and you can only hope that your partner steps up his/her game, or you must be open to meeting someone else who has the qualities you desire.

To break down the manifestation process:

1. Name It: Be absolutely clear about what you want to manifest.

2. Claim It: Feel what it will feel like once it has become your reality.

3. Own It: Focus on that feeling day and night, and be grateful that it is already done.

Whenever doubt creeps into your mind, go back to the feeling of already having what you want. Say to yourself, "**Already Done**." Once you've convinced yourself that it's already done, there is no reversing the process; it must come into manifestation. This is also called "conscious creation."

We, as human beings, are always creating our experiences, usually on an unconscious level. When you consciously start creating that which you wish to experience, life suddenly becomes a whole lot more interesting!

First, you start creating things just because you learn that you can. Then you come to realize some of the things you've created are working against you rather than for you. Sometimes we create such a mess, it takes time to unravel it all, and during the process, the thought of creating anything else becomes more work than it's worth. This shows up as confusion or a lack of desire. You just don't know what you want, so you don't want anything but to be left alone. Once the air clears, you'll come back to yourself with more wisdom and more clarity of choice. Then you begin again to consciously create your experiences but from a place of priority, and not just for fun.

The three steps outlined above for the manifestation process are simple. Yet, the mind is a powerful thing, and the subconscious mind is even more powerful than the conscious mind. The subconscious wants to keep you safe, to preserve the human species. Keeping you safe means keeping you limited to what's familiar and not reaching into the unknown. The unknown territory is where your dreams live so you've got to go there if you want to live an amazing life.

It can be difficult to rid ourselves of the limitations the subconscious mind places on us, but we can easily expand those limitations to include our desires. We can reprogram the subconscious mind to feel safe with our new choices. We do this with what I call the Power of VAM (Visualization, Affirmation, and Meditation).

VISUALIZATION

What the mind can conceive, it can achieve. Always start with the end in mind. What do you want to have, be, or do? See the end result as already accomplished. Run a vivid movie in your mind, one that includes as many of the five senses as you can deliver. What are the surroundings of the achievement? Who is involved; what is being said or done? What are the sounds and smells? What are the objects around you, and what do they feel like when touched? Get involved with the achievement, feel it, sense it, know it is already done. Run this mental movie, being fully involved and connected to the results each night just prior to sleep. This will give your subconscious mind something to work on during dream state. Keep a dream journal.

To learn more, check out the book "Creative Visualization" by Shakti Gawain. It's a classic and one of my favorites. If you're familiar with the work of Vishen Lakhiani, Mindvalley founder, he offers a beautiful technique for using creative visualization for healing.

AFFIRMATIONS

Your words have power. They can heal you or hurt you. Whatever you attach to the phrase "I am" becomes your experience, as you've just named it as you and claimed it for yourself. So think again before you say, "I'm broke." "I'm fat." "I'm tired." "I'm sorry." Also, whatever you speak out loud is spoken THROUGH you as though it is spoken TO you. So, if you call someone stupid, the subconscious mind computes "stupid." It does not distinguish who is stupid. Therefore, you have just called yourself stupid. This, in my opinion, is the universe's way of helping us wake up to the fact that we are all one. You can't harm another without hurting yourself in the process. That's the universal law of "What you put out, you get back" or "You reap what you sow."

In order to consciously create your experiences, you must consciously choose your words, words that empower your vision rather than weaken your vision. We do this by affirming the results we want to create. **Name it, claim it, and own it.**

1. Name it by being clear about what you want.

2. Claim it by attaching "I am" or "I have."

3. Own it by stating it in present tense as though it is already done.

Examples:

- I am healthy, wealthy, and wise.

- I am enjoying my new home.

- I am in love and loved by my perfect mate.

- I am grateful for my healed back.

- I have everything I need to succeed.

- I am living an amazing life.

Some folks can't get into saying "I am" if they are truly feeling the opposite. For instance, it may be difficult to say, "I am healthy" when you feel like a truck just ran over you. In this case, you might say, "I am 'willing' to be healthy." You can say, "I am grateful for the health I have."

Just remember to be conscious of your thoughts, and especially conscious of what you speak out into the universe. Whatever you put out there must return to you multiplied – that's the law. Multiply only good vibes.

MEDITATION

The final part of the power of VAM is meditation. There are a thousand or more ways to meditate. When I speak of meditation, it's not a traditional technique, it's more about taking the time to stop and listen to the still small voice within.

When you combine visualizing your goal with affirming it, the only thing left to do is listen for guidance to know your next step. This goes back to setting your intention and following your intuition.

Most people set goals and stop there. They don't take the time to listen to know what to do next. Stop and listen! You will be shown what to do, when to do it, and how to do it to achieve your goals. Make it a practice to sit for 15-20 minutes daily, preferably in the morning, for guidance throughout the day.

Make an appointment with yourself each morning to sit and visualize your goals, then write out your affirmation, and sit in silence to listen for guidance. If you don't receive guidance, it's okay. Make it a habit to sit each day, and you will start to develop your intuition and eventually begin to hear what Spirit is telling you. Review the chapter on "Allowing Grace."

If you journal your thoughts after, or even during your meditative sitting, you will begin to see a pattern of guidance developing. Journaling is one of the greatest tools for measuring your progress and personal growth.

> *Be Still and Know!*

Shift from Goddess to Queen

Now, what does mystical manifestation have to do with being a Lady? It carries a lot of weight when you can command your world by being able to manifest your desires with less stress and struggle. You live your life with more grace and ease.

The first step in taking on the manifestation process as a Lady is to know yourself as a Goddess and a Queen, and to embrace and embody all those feminine qualities.

The Goddess is flowing and easygoing, while the Queen is clear and focused. The Goddess asks, while the Queen commands. There is a beautiful and healthy balance here.

You may want to review the very first chapter, "Keep Calm and LadyUp" where I display **the many qualities of the feminine**. The Pleaser (goddess qualities), the Leader (queen qualities) and the Lady (goddess-queen qualities).

Goddess-Queens move from a place of grace. Most people create their world haphazardly, creating a lot of drama for themselves and all those around them. We are here to be conscious creators, focused and clear about our intentions.

You must realize your Goddess qualities and yet stand as a powerful Queen who transforms herself into a Lady at will. You are not someone who shows up as a constant "ruler" and commander, but one who can relax and be seductive as well as childlike and innocent by nature. Learn to possess all the qualities of the feminine and know how to shift from one to the other at any given moment with grace and ease. It's difficult for a man to label such a woman because she is forever changing, and that's a mystery to most men. Real men who are not threatened by the feminine find a real woman extremely enchanting and long to be in her presence. In a conversation with a male friend years ago, we were talking about men with multiple women. He said, "Why would I need more than my wife? It would take me a lifetime to just get to know her." A wise man indeed.

So how do you shift energies without being regarded as irrational and psychotic? You first know who you are, and you remain grounded in who you are. A Queen is good at this. She is clear about who she is and what she wants. She knows herself, including:

1. Her needs,
2. Her values,
3. Her boundaries, and
4. Her standards.

What Are My Emotional NEEDS?

(Beyond the needs of survival)

Some examples of emotional needs might be:

Acceptance	Accomplishment	Acknowledgment
Love	Respect	Caring
Clarity	Comfort	Understanding
Control	Value	Victory
Honesty	Order	Peace
Power	Recognition	Safety
Responsibility		

My emotional NEEDS (to feel alive) are:

_____ _____ _____

_____ _____ _____

_____ _____ _____

What Are My Personal VALUES?

Some examples of personal values might be:

Adventure	Beauty	Inspiring/Influencing Others
Contributing	Creativity	Learning/Discovery
Knowing My Feelings	Leadership	Mastery
Pleasing Others	Pleasure	Relating to Others
Sensitivity	Spirituality	Teaching

My personal VALUES (what's important to me) are:

_____ _____ _____

_____ _____ _____

_____ _____ _____

What Are My BOUNDARIES?

My personal BOUNDARIES (to feel safe/be comfortable) are:

_____

_____

_____

_____

_____

_____

_____

What Are My High STANDARDS?

My higher STANDARDS (to be happy) are:

_____

_____

_____

_____

_____

_____

_____

Once you are clear about who you are, your needs, values, boundaries and standards, your every desire, request, and command will be based on these qualities. With this type of clarity, your needs will be met more gracefully.

Knowing yourself, you now have the flexibility to shift from Goddess to Queen at will. You can decide if the situation calls for the Goddess energy to be sweet and seductive, or if it calls for the Queen to be clear and focused. You get to decide, and others will follow your lead. You are the world, and your energy creates your experiences. Shift as you may, but be graceful in doing so.

Use Your Magic Wand
(Funny, I always want to put an "a" after the word "Wand")

I didn't attend a traditional college. Instead, I spent 4 years studying at Thomas Institute of Metaphysics in Los Angeles. I learned about things they don't teach you in school, unless you're attending Harry Potter's school. If you know anything about being a mystic, you know that once you learn to use your powers, you can become very dangerous, not only to others, but also to yourself.

We've got enough crazies in the world today without teaching everyone how to sling a magic wand at someone. When the book and the movie _The Secret_ was released, I was excited, then I went, oh crap! Who will teach these people how to be responsible with their energy? Since there weren't a lot of true metaphysicians out there teaching the Law of Attraction, most people didn't really understand it and simply wrote it off as hocus-pocus. Yay!!!

You don't have to be a mystic to understand and use the Law of Attraction. You just have to use the power of VAM (Visualization, Affirmation, and Meditation) as mentioned above, but be consistent; don't give up. Most people give up right before the energy pops through into the physical realm, creating their desires. Stay focused until you can "FEEL" it and you will have it. Yes! It's that simple.

Simple as it may be, we have powerful minds. And, the mind thinks it needs to be physically productive. It needs something to do – always! You may have heard, "An idle mind is the devil's playground." If your thoughts are not supporting your dreams, they are working against you. This is why positive affirmations are important – they keep your active mind positive and on track.

Another way to keep our minds focused on the goal is to use tools, giving your mind and you some sort of physical expression. These tools I refer to as Magic Wands. The real magic they work is getting you out of your own way!

My favorite magic wand is a pointed clear quartz crystal. Crystals magnify energy and the clear quartz help to bring about clarity. You can use the crystal and point/direct the flow of energy in any direction you want. It works, and it's amazing!

Always feel the crystals prior to purchasing one. Avoid online ordering, unless you're extremely intuitive and the crystal calls out to you from the printed page. Select a crystal and hold the crystal in your non-dominant hand and you will know if it's the right one for you. It will immediately begin to heat up in response to your body temperature and start blending your energy for magnification.

It may take a moment, but if you don't feel anything rather quickly, put it down! Move on to the next crystal.

Once you have found your crystal, your magic wand, you may want to charge it by setting it outside overnight when there's a full moon. Crystals love the full moon energy and really soak it up! They also enjoy the sun's energy, so you can set it out on a bright sunny day to get fully charged, or recharged as well.

When your crystal is charged, use it for healing. Point the crystal to any part of your body that needs healing and state your intention clearly. Using an affirmation is powerful. Feel the energy of the crystal vibrating in your hand as you keep it pointed to the area of the body needing the energy. Know that dis-ease comes from blocked energy. Crystals clear energy blocks so that healing can occur easier and faster.

When your bank account is low, focus your crystal on the money you have and state your intention in the form of an affirmation. Example: "I am grateful for the money flowing into my bank account right now." "I am abundant and wealthy in all ways." "Money comes to me in ways, expected and unexpected." Make up your own positive affirmation. Then give thanks for the answered prayer. Repeat whenever doubt creeps in.

Whatever you need, allow your crystal, your magic wand, to work its magic for you. Be creative, but be safe. Be careful what you ask for.

When you've used your crystal for healing, you may want to recharge it by having it sit outside overnight again. Even on the dark of the moon, it will recharge and be ready for your next use. Never allow others to handle your crystal – it is attuned to your energy and is there to serve you. Should someone accidentally handle your crystal, recharge it again to clear it.

EXERCISE:

My very favorite process is one I learned over 40 years ago at Thomas Institute of Metaphysics. I've modified it over the years, but I still use it today to empower my mind and my thoughts as needed. It's using my crystal wand and working with a seven-pointed pyramid energy grid.

Tools Needed: Sheet of paper, marker, clear quartz crystal with a point, a small photo (headshot) of yourself, and a clear intention for what you wish to manifest.

1. Draw 7 large triangles/pyramids with the points all touching in the center of the paper. (*Think very large pie (big circle) with 7 slices*).

2. Place the photo of yourself in the center. Now there are 7 pyramids pointed directly at you! You just have to activate them. This is POWERFUL!!!

3. You are the center of your universe, and you are the creator. KNOW THIS. Now with your desires in mind, take your crystal (your magic wand) point it at your photo and state your desires. This is most powerful if stated as a positive affirmation in present tense. Example: "*I am happy, healthy, and living an amazing life*." State it with conviction! Command your world with gratitude that it is already done! Feel good about it! Own it! Know that it's already done!

4. Now utilizing your crystal wand, direct that energy out into the universe by tracing the lines of each pyramid, all three sides of each one separately, while repeating your affirmation out loud.

It does not matter which pyramid you begin outlining, but you must start tracing the lines, moving the intention out from the center, from you, and into the universe for manifestation, and then bringing the energy back around to you to receive it. Once you are back to your starting place, you can go around again and again, until you feel complete. Two or three times is usually sufficient to set the energy in motion. However, some deeper desires may require more rounds before you feel complete.

GET CREATIVE

This process of outlining each pyramid is encapsulating the energy inside the structure and pointing it (channeling it) directly to you multiplied seven times over!

An added bonus would be to identify each pyramid with your intention. If you want to manifest a partner in your life, you might label each pyramid with a quality, empowering that quality and bringing it directly to you through this process. Another idea is to use each section as a part of your body that may need attention. Notice you can color the grid below to represents the colors of the chakras and it can be used for healing or balancing your body's energy centers. You could use each section as a different part of your work or career. Each section could be used to identify and empower your family circle.

Reminder: This is powerful, so get creative, but be clear.

Be careful what you ask for, you just might get it!

Place your photo in the center.

Point your crystal and state your intention.

Begin to outline each pyramid, and follow the arrows.

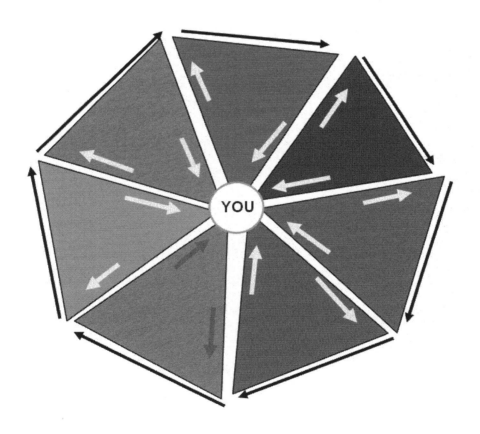

Be the Power You Possess

It's one thing to have power; it's another to "BE" the power. When the late and amazing Yolanda King hired me as her Life Coach, I asked what she needed. She said, "I'm a powerful woman, but I'm not an empowered woman."

Being powerful means you are getting power from outside of yourself. When a speaker is talking before an audience, if it's a deadbeat group, the speaker can fall flat unless they are an empowered speaker, one who can lift the room. The same holds true for musicians. If the crowd is alive, the music is jamming. If the crowd is sleepy, the musicians must look to their own power to raise the energy and bring life.

You are empowered when energy is generated from within and depends on no one or nothing outside of yourself to lift you or carry you. An empowered Goddess uplifts the world, an empowered Queen controls the world. An empowered Lady owns the world.

Just like anything else, if you want more power, name it, claim it, and own it. You have an undeniable inner power. The more you stand in this power and become it, the more powerful and empowered you become.

Years ago, I had the great pleasure of attending a week-long workshop entitled, "The Mystical Manifestation Process," led by an African Mystic, Ishmael Tetteh. Brother Ishmael taught us to manifest our desires by "having" whatever we wanted. He says you must first "have yourself, then the elements, and then your desires."

> *Mystical Manifestation Process:*
> *Have Yourself, The Elements, then Your Desires.*

This was his way of teaching us to be and own the power we possess. It goes like this:

1. **Have "Yourself"**
   a. Own your body, its parts, and all that you are.
   b. State each part's importance to you separately.
   c. Give thanks for each part separately.

2. **Have "The Elements"**
   a. Own the sun, the moon, the earth, and all the elements.
   b. State their importance to you, each one separately.
   c. Give thanks for having each one separately.

3. **Have "Your Desires"**
   a. Own your desires, each one separately.
   b. State the importance to you of each desire separately.
   c. Give thanks for having each one separately.

Example:
Have Yourself:

I have my body.

It takes care of me, supports me, and brings me great joy and pleasure.

I have my body.

I give thanks for my body.

I have legs.

They carry me, transport me wherever I need to go, and they are strong.

I have legs.

I give thanks for my legs.

I have _____ (repeat for any other body part that comes to mind).

Have the Elements:

I have the stars.

They provide light at night, and they bring me hope of tomorrow.

I have the stars.

I give thanks for the stars.

I have the earth.

It gives me life, it gives me food, water, and shelter. It protects me.

I have the earth.

I give thanks for the earth.

I have _____ (repeat for any other elements that come to mind).

Have Your Desires:

I have a new car.

It takes me wherever I want to go. It protects me and my family. It is beautiful.

I have a new car.

I give thanks for my new car.

> *I am amazing, and I am the power I possess.*

I HAVE	IT IS IMPORTANT *because*	BLESS IT (Give Thanks)
Have Your BODY		
Have The ELEMENTS		
Have Your DESIRES		

Again, our minds need to feel productive. Using a crystal wand or the process above are just two very powerful ways to allow the mind to work its magic and support you in achieving your desires.

My mother was a voodoo queen. I grew up watching her work her midnight magic. She taught me her secrets. Yet, even as a young child, I couldn't understand why anyone would spend money on candles and other objects to create magic. Why not just "have" what you want?

I was a Licensed Spiritual Counselor/Practitioner with the Agape International Spiritual Center for over 12 years. In order to become licensed, you had to first complete 4 years of study, including field work in the community. It turned out to be a great experience for me. However, in the beginning I fought the teachings like crazy. We were taught a 5-step process for prayer (*aka Spiritual Mind Treatment*) in order to manifest the desired outcome. I had one step, and that was to know, beyond a shadow of a doubt, that what I wanted was already done. I only needed to want it, allow it, receive it, and on to the next!

The first of the 5-step process is "Recognition," to recognize that there is a God or Universal Intelligence. Step two was "Unification," to know that you are part of this Universal Intelligence. Step three was "Realization," to know that what you want is already done in the mind of God. Step four was "Thanksgiving," to be grateful for the answered prayer. And then step five, "Release," letting go so that the universe can do its thing on your behalf.

Why did I suddenly need a 5-step process? I only needed step 3, realizing it was already done. Today, whatever it takes for me to know that it is already done, that is my process. It all depends on our faith, our belief that we can actually have what we want. If we have little faith, it takes longer because we have to build our faith, our consciousness to the point of receiving. If we already know it's ours before we even ask, time stands still, space opens up, and miracles happen. Bam! Mystical Manifestation!

In summary, I share all of this with you because, as a mystic and a Lady, you only need name it, claim it, and it is yours. Time is a man-made concept, so if it takes a long time to achieve your dreams, you've bought into the idea that time matters. A miracle is what happens when time and space come together in an instant. You have the power to allow this to happen. Allow it — you deserve it!

Chapter 5 – Mystical Manifestation

Personal Assessment

Shift from Goddess to Queen:

_____ I know that the clarity of my consciousness and the intensity of my feelings create my world.

_____ I truly understand that my feelings create the fuel that moves energy into manifestation.

_____ I use the power of VAM (Visualization, Affirmation, and Meditation) to focus my mind.

_____ I now practice Mystical Manifestation = I Name It, I Claim It, I Own It. Done!

_____ I can easily shift from Goddess to Queen because I know my Needs, Values, Boundaries, and Standards.

_____ Each year, on my birthday, I am committed to raising my Standards.

Use Your Magic Wand

_____ I always remember to do away with doubt by declaring, "Already Done."

_____ I have a magic wand and I am working with the Energy Grid to help focus my attention.

Be the Power You Possess

_____ I know how to affirm that "I Am" and I now practice affirming "I Have."

_____ I know that the Spirit I trust is not outside of myself. I know that the power of the Spirit is within me.

Notes to ponder and share with others

What's your deepest desire? Don't be shy, don't be afraid.

Name It, Claim It and Own It!
Right Here and Right Now.

Let your inner Mystic go wild!

Chapter 6
Building Happy, Healthy Relationships

Love Without Reason
Don't Slay the Dragon
Become a Master Receiver

Who Am I?

By Wanda Marie

We are one - We are love
We are together in this dream
Where daytime is a lifetime and
Nighttime is the end.

Who am I – A soul lost in the world of the unknown
Feeling full of life while inspired by death
Free to believe yet afraid to know who I am
Who am I?

Who are you? In all your uniqueness
Expressing illusions and experiencing reasons
Judging all – including self
Having it all but accepting less
Who are you?
Who am I?

Who are they?
Creating realities out of dualities
Finding fault in truth, power in money, and love in fear
Who are they?
Who are you?
Who am I?

They are us and we are them
Together as one we learn to be no longer lost in this dream
Where daytime is a lifetime and nighttime is the end.

Chapter 6: Building Happy, Healthy Relationships

LOVERS

He offered me an orange. Innocent at only 17. He was 21 and well-versed in the art of seduction. We're alone in his apartment. The Barry White song playing in the background "Hang On In There Baby" should have been a clue. He peeled the orange for me. I accepted it, took several bites and the juices ran down my fingers and my hand which he began to wipe away with tender gentle kisses. Those sweet kisses led to a shower together and 9 months later, a bouncing baby boy. He had promised I wouldn't get pregnant my first time – I trusted him. He lied.

It took him another nine plus months to convince me to marry him. I thought he was feeling sorry for me, so I kept saying no. I finally gave in to his persistence and wedding bells rang. He became husband number one.

I don't believe God would put a billion people on a planet and say you must find "the one" and once you do, you can only be intimate with that one person. That would be like going to an amazing buffet with all sorts of foods and desserts but saying, you have to pick one item for life.

My then husband felt differently. He said I was the one for him, and the only one for life. Yet, I made him agree that if at any point in our marriage he became attracted to another woman, he would talk to me before acting upon it. He agreed. Two kids and 20 years later, we divorced over mistrust and his infidelity. I've now been remarried to husband number two for more than 23 years.

> *The key to a happy, healthy relationship is trust and communication.*

PARENTS

Ladies, when you can say, "No" to your mother, you have reclaimed your power and have become your own person. It took me years. With a husband and two small children, I continued to do everything I could for my mother. She was a functioning alcoholic most of the time. Those times when she crossed the line, she became dangerous, not to herself, but to everyone around her.

She ended up losing everything and having to move in with me and my family. I laid down the rules. No drinking in my home. Violence will not be tolerated around my two small children. I will protect them at all costs.

It wasn't long before I had to have her removed from my home. I watched the police escort her away as tears rolled down my cheeks. My husband asked how could I put my own mother out on the streets. My response was, "It's not easy, but it's necessary."

She lived on the streets as a homeless person for approximately two years and then finally got her life together. We enjoyed an amazing mother-daughter relationship for many years before she passed away at the young age of 66. I had to be strong and say no to my mother's behaviors.

> *The key to a happy healthy relationship is having boundaries that you have the courage to enforce.*

CHILDREN

I arrived home from work to find a young girl climbing out of my 14-year-old son's bedroom window. I headed her off in the driveway. "Hi, I have one question for you. You're skipping school right now. Tell me, what do you want to be when you grow up?" Silence. I stepped aside and she passed on by. Inside the house, the smell of marijuana greeted me as I opened the door to my son's room. I announced, "This can't happen again." It happened again. I announced, "Third time and you no longer live here."

It happened a third time. "You have to leave, right now." Without speaking, he packed his backpack and left the house. I watched him walking away, down the street. Once again, tears rolled down my face from the pain of standing my grounds.

He ended up living with his older brother for years. He's in his early 40s now with a beautiful wife and three amazing children. We enjoy a deep, loving mother-son relationship.

I had to be clear enough to raise the standards for my living situation.

> *The key to a happy healthy relationship is raising your standards and teaching others to honor them.*

PEOPLE

Your family members are your greatest teachers. Don't pass up an opportunity to learn from them. Too many women leave the nest and don't want to deal with their family issues. So, they eventually create those same issues with other people, their chosen family.

Learn to be a great communicator. Set boundaries to protect yourself until you no longer need boundaries and you are ruling your court. Raise your standards and command respect from everyone, regardless of their title, rank or authority. Be the Queen.

> *How you handle the relationships in your life determines the quality of your life.*

Love Without Reason

I've always heard about so-called "unconditional" love, but I never believed it to be possible. After all, we all need each other. We would never survive alone. Therefore, if we need each other, our love must be based on our needs.

But then one day, I heard Byron Katie say, "I love my husband and he has nothing to do with it." WOW! That meant that she chose to love him, regardless. When you are at choice, you are empowered.

When I coach women on dating, I tell them not to "fall" in love, but to "step" into love gracefully. Don't rush in – only fools rush in.

When we as women are hurt by men, it's hard to get over it. It's hard because we are wired to think of men as provider and protector. When they don't live up to the role, we get hurt. We also get hurt because we expect so much from them in return for our love. When we choose to love a friend, we don't expect as much, just some quality friendship time. It's different.

When we are at choice and we decide to love someone for no reason at all, we are empowered. When we love someone "because" of what they can do for us, they are empowered. They have the power because they can simply decide to no longer do for us what makes us happy. This creates anger when we don't get what we want. Anger is a final attempt to control a situation. If you are trying to control something, you are not empowered, you are using force, not grace.

What if you decided that you don't need anything in return from those you give your love to? How powerful would your world be?

EXERCISE:

1. Make a list of a few people currently in your life that you love. Include some of your family members and friends. Not people you like or tolerate, but a few folks whom you truly love.

2. Then rate the intensity of your love for them on a scale of 1 to 10, with 10 being very intense feelings.

3. Now, list why you love them. What specifically do they do for you to make you love them the way you do?

Name	How much?	Reason (what do they do for you?)

4. Close your eyes and feel your love for the first person on your list. Think of what they do to earn your love. Now, imagine they are no longer being or doing this very thing. How does this make you feel? Do you still feel love for them? Has the intensity of your love lessened? To what degree/level?

Note: When we base our love on these spoken or unspoken conditions, it's not authentic love – it's a complicated compromise. When we love just *because we've decided to love, it's authentic and true. <u>No compromise is necessary</u>. It's powerful!*

5. Close your eyes again and image that person standing before you broken, in pain and needing something from you. Allow the nurturing qualities of the Goddess to come forth and comfort that person, regardless of what they've done or what has happened to them. Allow yourself to feel compassion for them and extend your heart. Love them. They need your love right now. Here's a beautiful saying and unfortunately, I don't know the author: *"Love me when I deserve it least; that's when I need it most."*

Note: No one is perfect, we are all broken in some way. When we can look to the parts of ourselves and others that are not perfect, we are better able to love them for who they are, without judgment and without expecting anything from them. We are the nurturing Goddess, we can do this with a grateful and open heart. We know that love heals and we are willing to heal those we love and see them whole, perfect, and complete.

6. Now move on to the next person on your list and repeat steps 4 and 5. Continue until you have completely shifted from loving each person by compromise to loving each person with true compassion.

Many women use their love as a means of controlling others. If others don't do what she wants, she will withhold her love. This is what women do, not Ladies. If a Lady has decided to love you, it's regardless of your acts or actions. If you change your ways, she may distance herself from you, but she will not stop loving you because you've changed or stopped serving her.

I enjoy discussing the <u>five love languages</u> with couples. This classic book by Dr. Gary Chapman is a wonderful guide to show each person's preference. Just in case you're wondering, the five love languages are: (1) words of affirmation, (2) acts of service, (3) receiving gifts, (4) quality time, and (5) physical touch.

My love language (preference) is acts of service. Yes, I'm such a Queen! Don't tell me; show me! When someone speaks my love language, I automatically love them – they are awesome! However, I'm very aware and careful not to become attached to the act. Anyone who naturally performs acts of service for another is a giver. Givers are angels and I love all givers, just for being who they are. So if they give to me, and suddenly stop for whatever reason, I just continue to love them for who they are.

It's fun to know your love language, but don't get caught up in what others are doing for you. Keep it real. Love them for who they are, not what they have to offer. Stay in your power.

Don't Slay the Dragon

With all types of relationships, it's difficult when you have expectations and to stay calm when those expectations are not met. We, as strong women, don't hesitate to slay the dragon when relationships get crazy. It goes crazy, and we go crazy! It doesn't matter if it's a romantic relationship, friendship, working relationship, or a relationship with our children, our parents, etc. If our expectations are not met, we can get a little crazy. This is because we are controlling, not commanding.

If you've ever been married and divorced, you learned a lot! It's as though the marriage was training camp for the real world. My second marriage is so much easier and grounded. There is less drama, and not just because we're older and wiser, but because we just don't care about all the little things. It's like having the first baby and you're paranoid because it burped while laying on its back. Then with the second or third child, you're just glad it burped, period. Experience is priceless. Learning to be a Lady takes training and experience so that when things get crazy, you don't get crazy. It's about **balancing power and grace**.

We don't want to slay the dragon – we want to build happy, healthy relationships with everyone in our court. We're usually a bit harder on romantic relationships. When coaching couples, one of the tools I like to refer them to is the four agreements. There's also a fifth agreement, but I've decided I really like sticking to the four.

The four agreements: (1) Be impeccable with your word, (2) don't take anything personally, (3) don't make assumptions, and (4) always do your best. These are from "The Four Agreements" by Don Miguel Ruiz, which I highly recommend reading.

When everyone in the relationship has a foundation they can agree upon, there's less struggle and drama. Not everyone will keep the agreements, but it helps as a guide to get back on track sooner rather than later.

I've found that one of the hardest things to do is to avoid making assumptions. We make assumptions based on history, which means we're not living in the moment. Assumptions have their foundation in trust. We trust the past more than the unknown future. If s/he hurt you once, you feel you can't trust that s/he won't hurt you again? However, you think that if you slay the dragon, cut them off from your love, s/he can never hurt you again. But the problem is that you are really hurting yourself.

If you cut someone off from love, you cut yourself off. The greatest power we have is the power to love. Love flows through us to others. When you cut off the flow, a backup happens within your own energy system. This backup usually shows up as fear, the opposite of love. When you don't allow love to flow through you, fear grabs hold of you and won't let go until you open the flow of love again.

So how do you learn to trust again, to love again, once you've been betrayed? I was on a trip to Egypt with a spiritual group and a few of us decided to go shopping. We found ourselves in a perfume shop. The salesman said to one of the male members of our group, "Wear this and the women will be all over you. Trust me." The guy in our group replied, "I don't need to trust you. I trust God." This is what I say to anyone who has ever been hurt and shut down. You don't need to trust people – you only need to trust that which created you, that which is guiding and directing you. Does this mean you'll never be hurt again? No, but what it does mean is that you will get back up on your feet quickly and be open to love again. It means you won't continue to do damage to yourself by stopping love from flowing; you'll be open to finding another, someone more worthy of your love, someone who is eager and willing to return your love.

You are always guided and directed. Often, we get hurt because we ignore the warning signs, the red flags. We must learn to stop ignoring our guidance. No matter how sweet s/he may seem, or how odd the situation, trust your guidance first!

When I met my current husband, we decided we would commit, not to each other, but to "LOVE." We decided that we really wanted to know love and that we would assist each other in this process. We had only known each other about three months before deciding to lease a house and move in together. We knew nothing about each other, only that the passion was there, but we wanted more. Our commitment was to not run away for six months, no matter what. We were smart enough to realize that with every relationship, there are rough spots and it's easy to run away when you hit one. We signed a six-month lease and were committed to sticking it out for the term of the lease to see what would unfold in our relationship.

The first couple of months were great. We were in lust. After that, we were in hell! But we could not run away – we had to talk through it, work through it, and find a way to live together until the lease expired. With lots of long talks late into the night, and me swearing, and him being patient, we got through it. We moved through all of our yucky patterns and into a place where it was safe to love. It was tough, but we made it through. We found love in each other and for each other. We didn't know each other well enough to really trust each other, but we trusted love and love led the way.

Did I slay the dragon? Oh yeah! More than once! Was he man enough to hang in there? Oh yeah! I've always been a Queen and it takes a real King to handle my energy.

He was amazing during my slaying years. I've since learned to be more of a Lady, filled with more grace.

The Blueprint of We

Another wonderful tool for couples to learn to coexist in harmony is "The Blueprint of We," referred to in the past as the **State of Grace Document** written by Maureen McCarthy. "*State of Grace*" – how appropriate to help us "LadyUp!" In the document, Maureen offers some powerful questions to ponder when things get crazy. Here are a few:

- What am I afraid of – including what am I afraid of really saying right now?

- What truths do I need to tell?

- What do I need right now?

- What do we each have to gain by ending this relationship?

- What do we each have to gain by continuing this relationship?

- What part does money play in this situation?

- Is there a power struggle going on between us?

- What do I appreciate most about you?

- What do I have to forgive myself and/or you for?

- Is it time to redefine or redirect this relationship?

- What is the deep-down knowing we each have about how this will eventually end up?

> *What deep and fearless questions do you Need to ask about your relationships?*

Remember, happy healthy relationships all start with open and honest communication. If one person is not willing to be open and honest, RUN! Run either to therapy together, or run away from each other. Save yourself some heartache.

Are you currently in a relationship with your king or queen companion/soulmate? If not, and you're looking, here's a mystical magical exercise that can help you attract your partner.

Exercise:

1. Awaken at the mystical hour of 3:00 a.m. when most are asleep.

2. Call in your soulmate with clarity and conviction: State, "I will know you when I see you because:

    a. You will be wearing _____ (*state whatever you decide that is distinctive and unmistakable, like a yellow feather in a hat.*)

    b. You will say to me (*create an unforgettable phrase*).

    c. You will show up in my life before the end of _____ this year (*or whatever season and year you feel is appropriate for your life*)."

3. Give thanks: "I give thanks for you being willing and ready to meet, and I give thanks to the Universe for bringing us together, as we are perfect for each other."

Do not set an alarm to wake up. If this process is for you, you will wake up automatically by setting an intention to do so. If it takes several days or weeks before you wake up, trust the divine timing of it all.

Do the Mystical Manifestation Process and "Have" the love of your life. Then set an intention to wake up at 3:00 a.m. for this process. Once you do the Mystical Manifestation Process, you may begin seeing the energy of attraction coming your way sooner than you realize!

Let go of all your pictures of what your soulmate is supposed to look like. You are only setting yourself up for disappointment. It is not always love at first sight. What matters most is the attraction your soul and his/her soul will share. If you are attached to your pictures, you may have a difficult time attracting your true soulmate – you will miss him or her because you are not looking for what is real. Know that he or she could be even more attractive than the pictures in your mind.

Create-A-Mate: Things to Know/Remember:

1 Become whole first. Females should use their masculine sides to provide and take care of themselves and males should use their feminine sides to nurture and support themselves.

2 Set your INTENT for exactly what qualities you want in a mate. Then focus on something else, another project, to let go so your intent can manifest. When you don't let go, it's like watching a cake bake. So many women who have trouble conceiving find they get pregnant once they go on vacation and stop trying so hard.

3 Be friendly and outgoing, and know that you are the prize for the right person.

4 Don't compromise – settling for unworthy people makes you unworthy of the right person.

5 Be clear, and ask yourself a couple of questions, (1) What do I need a mate for? And (2) How would having a mate change or benefit my life?

Know that when you have your soulmate, there will be fire! Women often think the soulmate experience is blissful, loving, and peaceful. Most of the time, it's fire! It's hot, it's awesome and amazing, and it can be dramatic and intense all at the same time. This is when you get to practice being a real Lady. Our natural tendency as a woman is to control and demand. Now you get to stand still and command that those around you respect your boundaries and uphold your standards so that you don't have to be so controlling. To command your world is to simply KNOW beyond a shadow of a doubt how things should be, and declare order in your court gracefully and lovingly.

One more thing: When you want to slay the dragon, look to your heart for more compassion. The next time someone pisses you off, realize they are doing the best they can with what they've got. I practice eternal forgiveness. When we truly understand oneness, we will never want to hurt anyone again.

Ladies, put down your sword. Trust that the Universe will protect you when you set your intention and follow your intuition.

Become a Master Receiver

I spend a great deal of time coaching women on becoming more empowered, to know what they want and be able to ask for it. And, then there's the piece of the happiness puzzle that always seems to be missing. It's called worthiness.

I honestly don't understand how anyone could be breathing and not know they are worthy of having what they want in life. I can only assume religious dogma has something to do with it, especially when some religions say that we're born sinners. If you believe in reincarnation, that may be true. However, if you believe in reincarnation, you must also believe in karma which says, we are not punished "for" our sins, we are punished "by" our sins. It's another way of saying "what goes around, comes around," either in this lifetime or another.

If you believe you are a sinner, you need to do whatever it takes to get over it. Repent, forgive, make amends, whatever you need to do, just do it. In order to have happy healthy relationships, you have to be in full alignment with giving and receiving. Most women do the giving part extremely well. But they are out of alignment unless they are also doing the receiving part equally as well.

We are given whatever we ask for, believe we can have, and allow to flow to us. The one thing that throws a wrench in the process is trying to control where it comes from. You can say you want more love, and hope and expect that your partner will deliver. If this is your only avenue for allowing more love, you may be disappointed. You must be open and allow what you want to come from not just expected, but unexpected, sources.

A spiritual teacher told her followers she wanted to build a free hospital for the poor. Her followers asked, "Where will the money come from?" She replied, "Wherever it is now."

At this point, you have gotten clear on the value of your time, you know you are beautiful and powerful, you have healthy boundaries and high standards, you know how to manifest what you want, including a mate if you so desire. Now, you must know that you are worthy of receiving everything your heart desires, and living an amazing life.

When I'm at choice between buying the blue shoes and the brown shoes, I remind myself that I can have both. Then, I usually decide more easily which ones to take home. Knowing and reminding myself I can have anything I want, helps me make decisions from a place of want rather than need. If you think you can't have something, you're entertaining lack. Need responds to lack by having you make unhealthy and sometimes desperate decisions.

> *Need responds to lack by having you make unhealthy and sometimes desperate decisions.*

When someone offers me a gift or offers to pay for lunch, etc., my response is, "Thank you, I receive all good gifts." Never ever shortchange yourself. If the Universe wants to give you something, it's usually done through another person. Why would you deny the Universe by not accepting your good just because you may not like or trust the delivery person?

Women have been programmed to think that if a man gives them something, they are expecting something in return. This is usually true, but not always. Before you refuse the gift, offer to engage in clear communication.

Before marrying my second husband, we were living together, and I was at the point of wanting to change careers. I was ready to shift from paralegal work to running my Life Coaching practice full time. My fear was giving up my salary-based security. He encouraged me to move forward and quit my job. Before I could do this, I needed to have a heart-to-heart conversation. What if I don't have enough clients? He was working every day and I would be working from home, so would he expect me to prepare dinner every night and clean the house (we had a housekeeper while I was working)? What were his expectations? We did a lot of talking and got very clear about how our lives would look if we had less income and I was home every day. I still didn't trust that he would be okay with the situation, but when he said, "I want to support you, let me be the man," I decided to trust, not him, but the Universe. I quit my job. Not only did he follow through on supporting us, but it improved our relationship as it gave him more purpose and a sense of pride.

In order to be a master receiver, you first must be a good receiver. We are anatomically built as receivers and men are built as givers. They give sperm, we receive the sperm, and turn it into a child. Back in the day, men would go hunting and bring home food, and women would receive it and turn it into a meal. We get a house and turn it into a home. Whatever raw materials we are given, we are born to make something wonderful from it. This is how we are naturally wired. If you don't allow yourself to receive, you block your own creativity.

EXERCISE:

For the next 30 days, practice being a good receiver. When given a gift, or if someone does something for you, make eye contact and say, "Thank you" with a smile. If you offer any other words, you are deflecting the gift and the giver. What you're really doing is thanking the Universe by way of the person offering the gift. If that's too difficult, you can say, "Thank you, I accept."

Sometimes just a couple more words can make it easier, but too many words defeat the gift. If opportunities don't present themselves for you to practice, create opportunities. Start dropping things in front of men. If they're gentlemen, they will pick things up for you. You'll get to make eye contact and say "Thank you" with a smile. Practice, practice, practice at least for 30 days. If needed, extend it to 60 days or more, until you feel that you've become a good receiver.

The Master Receiver

The Master Receiver does not need to say a word for words cannot convey the deep gratitude felt by a Master Receiver. There is an exchange of energy that is felt more than heard. The eyes pierce deep into the soul with acknowledgment for the giver, not the gift, for it is the giver that is most precious.

Most women can't even make eye contact when receiving a gift. This is the reason it's important to practice being a good receiver first.

When a queen is given something, does she make a big deal over it? No, she simply acknowledges the gift in gratitude for the giver.

If you're in a romantic relationship and your partner's love language is "words of affirmation," then you will want to honor that when receiving a gift from them. But, only until you have mastered the art of deep gratitude. Once you can look through a person and into their soul, I assure you, the words will only get in the way. That which is beyond words of affirmation is deep connection.

Since we know that what you give out you get back, the key to life is to give away the very thing you want to attract. A Master Receiver is a Master Giver. The more you give, the more you get — it's a Universal Law like gravity. What goes out from you, as a magnetic being, must return to you.

The Key to Life Is to Give Away the Very Thing You Want to Attract

I used to keep spare change in my car to give to the homeless standing with signs on the road or those who approached me in parking lots. I have to admit, I was judgmental and would not give to men. I felt that men should be providers, not asking me, a female, for money.

I soon got over it when one day, I was leaving my office heading for my car parked in a lot across the street from my office. I saw what seemed to be a homeless man walking along the sidewalk on the same side of the street where my car was parked. I knew we would be approaching my car about the same time, and I expected he would ask me for money. He looked to be in his mid-thirties, and his clothing was torn and dirty. He was sucking on a lollypop. We reached my car at the same time. He did ask if I could spare any change. I looked at him, caught his eyes and almost fell to my knees. I knew I had just seen Jesus, the son of God himself! I said, "sure," turned and unlocked my car, grabbed some change and turned around, and he was gone. The streets were clear and there was no place he could have hidden. He just vanished in thin air.

I instantly knew this experience was to heal my judgment about giving to men, or anyone. Some folks say not to give to the homeless because they will only use it to buy booze or drugs. That's not our concern; that's their business. Our business is to take advantage of the opportunity to give.

As Ladies, I wanted you to first understand and be aware of your boundaries. We can often give so much that we feel used or abused. When we give what we don't have, it often turns to resentment. When this happens the energy that is returned to us is hostile. We must give with an open heart, which means to give freely, without expecting anything in return. That means you give from a place of abundance, not from lack or need. This also means you are balanced so the energy that returns to you is also balanced.

It's super-important to know when to say, "No." Again, it's all about following your intuition. If it feels good, go for it – without judgment or concern. If there is doubt, stop! Trust yourself, regardless of the circumstances.

Sometimes we hesitate because we're not sure of what's needed. Ask for guidance and then proceed. Ask yourself, "Is this mine to do?" If you don't receive guidance, just be still. In cases of emergency, you will automatically and intuitively jump into action if it is yours to do so. Again, just trust yourself.

Start giving. Give at every opportunity that feels right, knowing that as you are blessing someone, you are being blessed ten times over. And, when you need something, don't be afraid to ask! You must also allow others that same opportunity to be a blessing for you, so they may receive their blessings ten times over as well.

Because I know this universal law so well, years ago, I set an intention for my life that anyone who gave me money for my services would be blessed in return. My clients are usually amazed at how their lives shift when working together. It's not so much about what I do – it's more about the giving and the receiving. My work is not in the process; it's infused with grace. We do go through the motion, the process, just to appease the busy mind for those who have yet to know the power of grace.

EXERCISE: For the next 30 days, look for opportunities to give. You can give of your time, your talents, your money, or other resources.

> **Money:** If you want more money circulating in your life, create a "spending plan," not a "budget." Budgets indicate limitations. If you have money, you are going to spend it for one thing or another, so why not do it consciously by creating a "spending plan." Within this plan, decide how much money you want to give away during the 30-day period. Then spread it out over the course of the month, giving some away each day or

each week. Look for opportunities to give and GIVE! Have fun with this.

Love: If you want more love circulating in your life, look for opportunities to love more. Love is love, it need not be romantic love. But, if you want romance, be more romantic. Compassion is love in action. Look for those in need of compassion and offer a listening ear or to help in any way you can. Help an elder put groceries in their car; that's love. Go feed the homeless – that's a demonstration of love in action. Donate old clothes. Help a friend in need. Call someone you've been thinking about and tell them you appreciate them. Say, "I love you" more often to those close to you. Practice a few random acts of kindness. Make a list of ways you can love more. Then over the next thirty days, decide what you will accomplish each day or each week to love more.

Whatever you want more of in your life, find ways to give more of that to others, to the world, and watch how it starts making its way back to you multiplied.

Be the gift you wish to receive.

I commend you for finishing this book. I know some of the exercises have been challenging and you may need to go back and review a few of them. The good news is that if you do not yet feel like a Lady, like your life has less stress and struggle and more grace and ease, know that you are well on your way. Just keep reviewing the exercises. Rinse and repeat until you know you've got this!

I'd like to leave you with this quick and simple assessment and affirmation for creating and living an amazing life.

Walking In Grace Questions:

1. What do I need to feel safe? _____

2. What am I resisting? _____

3. What am I afraid of? _____

4. What are the opportunities here? _____

5. What do I need to let go of? _____

6. Am I living in the present? _____

Affirmation:

I am a powerful and dynamic woman, filled with radiant beauty and grace. I know who I am. I am confident, wise, youthful, and poised. I am divinely guided in all that I do and say. My life is magical and everyone in my world is healthy, happy, and prosperous. I no longer need to be needed, I am whole, perfect, and complete right here and right now. My cup runneth over! And I am graceful enough to receive the overflow! I have an amazing life! Life is beautiful and so am I.

Chapter 6 – Happy, Healthy Relationships

Personal Assessment

Love Without Reason

_____ I am a master communicator. I never give the silent treatment. I never sweep things under the carpet. I'm brave enough to put it all on the table.

_____ I have healthy boundaries and I gracefully teach others how to honor them, creating peace and harmony for everyone in my court.

_____ I'm clear about the consequences for crossing my boundaries, and I have the courage to lovingly enforce my boundaries in all situations.

_____ I am committed to raising my standards every year on my birthday, raising them so high that boundaries become no longer necessary.

_____ I love everyone unconditionally by accepting them just as they are.

_____ I have eternal forgiveness for everyone because I understand they are doing the best they can with what they have, and we are one.

Don't Slay the Dragon

_____ I don't lead with my sword, but I know how and when to use it.

_____ I trust my instinct and never regret or feel guilty about having to slay the dragon.

_____ I always love first, listen second, and slay only if necessary. Even when I'm slaying the dragon, it is done with the utmost love.

_____ I know how to balance my power with grace.

_____ I honor the four agreements and insist that my partners do so as well.

_____ If I get hurt, I move on and love again because I don't put my trust in people, I trust the Universe to take care of me.

Become a Master Receiver

_____ I am a "Good" receiver. I always make eye contact and say, "thank you" with a smile.

_____ Every day I practice being a "Master" receiver by simply acknowledging gifts with a deep soul connection and smiling eyes – the Queen's way.

_____ I get that "receiving" is my job and I do it well.

_____ I know that giving is the counterpart to receiving and I am also a Master Giver. I give at every opportunity that feels right to me.

_____ I give without expecting anything in return. I know the real gift is in the giving.

_____ Whenever I feel it inappropriate to receive a gift, I try to negotiate options prior to rejection. If there are no viable options, I gracefully decline the gift, knowing it was not mine to receive.

_____ I realize that the Universe is abundant and is my source. Those who deliver the gifts are messengers and I am grateful to them for accepting the job. I never confuse the source with the messenger.

I am always fed, nurtured, supported, and empowered by all my relationships.

Notes to ponder and share with others

Conclusion

The Magic Behind Grace and Ease

Conclusion: The Magic Behind Grace and Ease

I've been told that I make life look easy. I always seem to get what I want, and whenever I get knocked down, which isn't too often, I get back up rather quickly. People have said my life seems magical.

I came to realize that I have truly created an amazing and grace-filled life for myself, a life that is easy and primarily drama-free. When I break down the components of how this works, there are three basic principles that make up this magical life of mine.

1. **Clear Vision.** 95% of the time I am super-clear about what I want in my life, and the experiences I want to have. When confusion happens during the other 5%, that's when drama comes alive. That's also when I go to my altar to get clear again. Sometimes I go to my altar once and done. Other times, it takes going daily before clarity arrives. But, clarity always comes and gets me back on track.

2. **Knowing Beyond Trusting.** We usually hope for something first, then we trust it will come, and finally, we know for sure it's happening. For everything in life, you must know it to have it. If you are trusting the Universe to deliver, it may be a while, but it will come if your faith is strong enough. However, if you already KNOW it's done, that knowingness collapses time and your future becomes your present reality. A miracle is not a special event. Miracles happen moment to moment when we are aligned with knowing. Hope separates you from your desires. Trust brings you closer. Knowing makes it real.

3. **This or Something Better.** I know that I'm guided and directed by something larger than my ego. Call it God, Higher Power, Universal Intelligence, whatever – it's bigger than you and I. Therefore, when I ask for something, I always end my prayer with, "This or something better." You may "think" you know what's best for you, but there is

always something greater, something beyond your imagination. Leave the door open for greatness to enter your life. If you live by this notion, at every disappointing occurrence, you will begin to immediately know that something better is on the way for you.

This puts your mind at ease. Even in the most painful or difficult situations – you can smile knowing that something better is happening to you, for you, and through you.

The magic behind a life filled with grace and ease comes from being totally clear about what you want, knowing it's possible, asking for it, and declaring, "This or something better."

When you know what you want, it's usually tied to your values. If you base all your decisions around your values, you will automatically have healthy boundaries and high standards. No one will be allowed to waste your time (you're on a mission). No one will be allowed to violate you (you will slay them instantly). You will gain freedom and respect at the same time for who you are as a true Lady. So, it's time to LadyUp!

My definition of a Lady is a woman with self-defined grace and fearless love. To "LadyUp" means to stand as a woman of power who commands her world with the grace of a Lady.

> *A Lady has all the amazing qualities of the Princess, the Goddess and the Queen, and she can shift between each within the blink of an eye.*

> *A Lady has self-defined grace, meaning she creates her own path and walks it with such dignity that she commands the respect of all those around her.*

> *She has fearless love, meaning she chooses love above all else and loves without reason. She does not use love as a weapon; she uses love to teach, nurture, and heal.*

Her life has less stress and drama because she lives by grace and ease. Her world is in order and surrounded by beauty. Time is always on her side because she plans wisely and teaches others to value her time.

She feels confident about the decisions she makes because she is connected to universal intelligence and sets her intention and follows her intuition.

She is passionate about life because she knows she's in charge of her court, her world.

She loves her body and never compares herself to anyone else. She knows that she is a unique work of art which could never be duplicated.

She is a Master Receiver and Giver. She receives with gratitude and gives with grace. There is never any judgment.

One thing that's important about being a Lady is allowing grace. When we can live life in complete confidence and surrender to our vision, we will be more at peace, we will experience more pleasure, we will be kinder to others, and we will attract more good into our lives.

How much good can you handle? How long can you stand being left out of the drama? How many ways can you be still and know that everything is okay? This is a daily practice. When you decide to up your game as a Lady, you will find it's not always easy, but it's always worth it. Clear vision is the first step. When you need to get clear and work your magic, you will need a special place to go and be still, your place of worship. Here's an idea for creating a sacred altar and preparing for prayer work.

Creating Your Sacred Altar

1. Find a location that "feels" right to you, where you can set up your altar and it will not be disturbed by others.

2. Clear the space by prayer and/or smudge with white sage.

3. Use stones from the earth to mark the four directions (north, east, south, west).

4. Place on the altar something representing the four elements:

   Earth: dirt or stones used for marking the directions

   Fire: candle for burning

   Air: incense for smoke

   Water: a small bowl for water

5. Include a picture of a sacred deity or a sacred symbol that has special meaning to you.

6. Include whatever else your heart desires, like your photo, maybe a picture of something you desire (*an object, but not another person*).

Preparing for Prayer or Ritual:

1. Clear the space each time before you begin by smudging with sage, or simply asking to be surrounded by White Light (deflects darkness).

2. Invoke (acknowledge) the four directions.

3. Place a fresh bowl of water on or near the altar.

4. Light a candle (colors can have influence).

5. Invite your Higher Power (Guardian Angel, Spirit Guides, etc.) to join you.

6. Pray, calling forth what you want, ask for guidance, for clarity, whatever you need.

7. Meditate and open to receive insights and answers. Remain in this space until it "feels" right to end the ritual. You may be moved to just sit and be still, or to sing, or chant, dance, or pick up a book and read something. Allow the energy to guide you.

Colors Vibrate –

Chose the right colors for your particular ritual/desires:

Red	survival, passion, drive
Orange	creativity, procreation
Yellow	willpower, direction, decisions
Green	love, healing, newness, growth, money
Blue	communications, understanding, expression
Indigo	psychic awareness, intuition, insight, clarity
Purple	wisdom, royalty, knowledge
White	purity, Christ Consciousness

There are a million or more different ways to get centered and call forth your desires – this is just one way. I only ask that you do not beseech or beg anyone for anything. Take the Queen's stance and command your world – you deserve your good – know this! When you become a beggar, you're coming from a place of need. Need affirms separation. Separation causes pain. Affirm, "Already Done." See it, feel it, taste it, smell it. Name it, claim it, own it, and give thanks for it!

The Universe responds to clear commands. The Universe rearranges itself to fit your idea of reality. That's a powerful statement – and a true statement. So, if your idea is that reality sucks, the Universe will confirm this for you. If your idea is that reality is awesome and life is good, the Universe will confirm this for you as well. You may not get to determine just how things will unfold in your life, but you can certainly determine the way you will respond and walk through life. Attitude is everything!

As a Lady, part of having your space in order is creating beauty. Beauty within itself is sacred and magical. Everyone responds to beauty. When you surround yourself with beauty, you will respond to life in a more positive way – and life will respond to you more favorably. Create beauty at every opportunity, especially with your altar.

As you work with your altar, begin to expand that energy to your entire living space. Although I have a place for meditation, my entire home is an altar. When people visit, they always comment on how good it feels to be in our home.

One Final Note: Be Successful and Help Others

They say it's lonely at the top. So take someone with you! No one ever became successful by themselves. We all need each other. The problem is that a lot of successful people use other people as stepping stones to make it to the top, and that's why they end up there all alone.

One of the greatest things you can do on your journey to success is to help others become successful. The key to success is to help others get what they want/need first. As you provide value to others, that value is returned to you multiplied in ways that are expected and unexpected!

Know what you want, pray a bold prayer, and turn your passion into profits. Don't be afraid to take risks – state your intention and follow your intuition.

If you are in business for yourself, raise your fees every year on your birthday. You are more valuable each year. You're older and wiser. Charge more so you can contribute more.

If you have issues around making money and building wealth, here's your assignment:

First, ask yourself these 2 questions:

1. Am I giving enough?

2. How can I create more value for others?

Second, complete each sentence that applies to you. Jot down the first response that comes to mind, as it's usually coming directly from your subconscious, that part of the brain on autopilot which runs our lives and our habits, and ultimately determines our life's experiences.

1. Money makes me feel safe because _____

_____

2. I don't trust money because _____

_____

3. I love money because _____

_____

4. I don't like money because _____

_____

5. I love the way I _____ money.

6. Money is a good source of _____ for me.

7. I am not comfortable receiving more than $_____ per week/month/year.

8. I am afraid of larger sums of money because _____

_____

9.   People with lots of money are usually _____ and
_____

10. I want more money so I can _____

11. I need more money so I can _____ and _____
and _____

12. The easiest way for money to come to me is _____
_____

13. The hardest way for me to get money is _____
_____

> *The Most Powerful Thing You Can Do Is "Be"*
>
> *The Most Wasteful Thing You Can Do Is "Beg"*

The LadyUp Creed to Live By

To stand as a woman of power who commands her world with the grace of a Lady

1.   We own our time and we're not afraid to charge for it.

2.   We no longer struggle; we command Order in every aspect of our lives.

3.   We bring and invite Beauty into our world with grace and ease.

4.   We honor and promote our Passion, for self-expression as well as for profit.

5.   We allow more Grace into our lives by setting our intention and trusting our intuition.

6.   We honor our bodies with extreme self-care and unconditional love.

7.   We are clear about who we are, always authentic, ready and willing to be seen.

8.   We easily shift between the feminine qualities of innocence, seduction, and mastery.

9.   We are not afraid of our power, for with it, we are wise and responsible.

10. Our Word is our wand and our sword – we can comfort the sick or slay the dragon.

11. We never withhold Love – we use it to teach, nurture, and heal.

12. We receive with grace and ease, and never negate a compliment, for we are Ladies.

> *Never Underestimate a LADY.*
> *She's a Playful Goddess and Fearless Queen.*

Final Notes to ponder and share with others

_____

_____

_____

_____

_____

_____

_____

_____

_____

_____

_____

_____

_____

_____

_____

_____

_____

About the Author

Wanda Marie Lapointe is the founder of Legacy Lifestyles LLC, a North Carolina company specializing in women's empowerment and business development. She is the author of "***Living Inner Peace: A Personal Guide to Greater Happiness,***" and co-author, with Yolanda King, on "***Embracing Your Power in 30 Days: A Journey of Self-Discovery and Personal Freedom***." Wanda has been a Certified Master Life & Business Coach, Trainer, and Inspirational Speaker for over 25 years. She enjoys speaking to women's groups on topics such as Finding Inner Peace, Embracing Your Power, and Building Your Dreams.

A deep connection to the spiritual essence of life since early childhood caused Wanda to study various western religions and eastern philosophies, cultivating her own spiritual foundation. She spent more than 12 years as a Licensed Spiritual Counselor and has traveled to the ancient land of Greece, celebrated Amma's (Mata Amritanandamayi) 50th birthday in Southern India, and meditated with spiritual leaders inside the Great Pyramids in Egypt.

Wanda has dedicated her life to helping women heal their lives and live their dreams. Learn more by visiting www.CoachWandaMarie.com or www.LadyUpNetwork.com.

Made in the USA
Columbia, SC
23 February 2022

56702228R00087